Linda—

Blessings

[signature]

SEXY christians

The Purpose, Power, *and* Passion *of* Biblical Intimacy

DR. TED ROBERTS & DIANE ROBERTS

BakerBooks

a division of Baker Publishing Group
Grand Rapids, Michigan

© 2010 by Ted and Diane Roberts

Published by Baker Books
a division of Baker Publishing Group
P.O. Box 6287, Grand Rapids, MI 49516-6287
www.bakerbooks.com

Printed in the United States of America

Library of Congress Cataloging-in-Publication Data
Roberts, Ted.
    Sexy Christians : the purpose, power, and passion of biblical intimacy / Ted Roberts & Diane Roberts.
        p.   cm.
    Includes bibliographical references (p.   ).
    ISBN 978-0-8010-1346-1 (cloth)
    1. Spouses—Religious life. 2. Sex—Religious aspects—Christianity. 3. Intimacy (Psychology)—Religious aspects—Christianity. I. Roberts, Diane, 1947– II. Title.
    BV4596.M3R635 2010
    261.8′357—dc22   2009040735

Contents

Foreword

The rumor started as a whispered story. I almost disregarded it as an urban legend, except I hoped it was true. It spoke of a church of a conservative, evangelical persuasion in which the pastor challenged people to look at sex addiction. The story suggested this pastor asked the entire church to have an ongoing discussion about sex and life as a committed Christian.

Next I met a few members of the church at various conferences who moved the story from whispered rumor to witnessed reality. They reported hundreds of church members attending groups for both men and women. Best of all, they said the participation profoundly enriched the entire congregational experience.

I hoped it was true because I knew the first person people will talk to about sex is their pastor. Many people are in recovery today because a pastor knew enough to get them help. Through the years, though, the church has had a hard time talking about human sexuality in terms of faith and love. Legalism and unfounded prejudice have generally won out. Still, it is in the faith context that many are likely to begin a journey toward healing.

Across denominations, the sexual scandals of pastors have reinforced shame and sexual negativity. Somehow, the lesson of the gospel about Christ coming for the wounded and struggling has been missed. Pastors are supposed to be perfect, with no struggles or defects. Yet Christ aimed all his parables at the Pharisees—the numb religious leaders who followed the law without the love. Their effort was to control God by perfect adherence to the rules, losing sight of his reaching out to them in relationship. In the midst of this negative arena, the idea of an innovative church and pastor on the horizon was heartening.

And then I met the pastor everyone was telling me about: Ted Roberts. In his own modest way, he told me of his efforts to reach out to people whose sexual wounds were seldom addressed in a faith context. I thought, *What a model for others!* So many churches and denominations could use this level of forthrightness.

No one who knows Ted will miss his Marine background and decisive style. His is the type of passion that can transform. But Ted is not without doubts or struggles, so he talks about them. No model existed for what he sought to do. The model he knew well was the Son of God, who was willing to persevere in love when all betrayed him, and the Son of Man, who was willing to break with codes and attitudes built on self-righteousness.

There's more. I have known many clergy who joined a sex addiction bandwagon without the study and diligence necessary to understand this complex problem. It takes investment and effort to understand how neuroscience is transforming our understanding of this illness and addiction in general. After that, further effort is required to know what really works. In clinical language we call this an *evidence-based approach*. If you immerse yourself in this effort, you have to confront much in yourself. Many want to skip that hard work. There are also those who fear religious leaders will focus on the sinful aspects of sexual addiction as opposed to the gigantic health problem it represents. And unfortunately, that has happened in some cases.

Ted has taken the time to learn what he needs to know in order to translate the depth of the challenge for his church, his denomination, and other believers. He has had the humility and the willingness to learn. I have witnessed over the last decade his effort to be prepared to do his work well and his recognition of a crucial truth: *when it comes to human sexuality, we must all continue learning.*

With all the various denominations and faith-based traditions, it is difficult to get a consensus on human sexuality. Similar barriers exist in the areas of clinical and academic science. Put another way, the spirit of the Pharisees can be found in any arena. Every major scientific breakthrough requires challenging dogmas. The church does not have a monopoly on self-righteousness. Whether everyone agrees does not matter. Having the conversation is vital. We know from studies of mental health, violence, culture, and government that the way men and women treat each other sexually and the way we raise our children shapes the future of society. On a planet that desperately needs openness and collaboration, the sexual conversation is clearly the most important one to have.

Recall the story of the Prodigal Son. This parable from the Gospel of Luke was told as instruction to those caught up in the law. The eldest brother's self-righteousness was a profound woundedness that prevented him from accessing the great love of God. Tim Keller, with succinct insight, points to the role of the father in the story. The father joyfully embraces his prodigal son and initiates the feast. The son is so filled with shame he feels unworthy, but the father welcomes him and helps him take a rightful place of grace. He also invites the eldest brother to the feast, but his self-righteousness prevents him from accepting his own rightful place. But the father keeps inviting them both.[1]

I see Ted Roberts as one of those people who invites us into the feast—the feast that celebrates human sexuality. Consider this book your invitation.

Patrick Carnes, PhD
Founder, International Institute for
Trauma and Addiction Professionals

Introduction

Good Morning America!

TED

"Hi, Dr. Roberts, I'm Monica." Her incredibly perky voice greeted me as though she knew me well. I held my cell phone slightly away from my ear as she continued. "I'm from *Good Morning America*!"

I hadn't grasped what was going on. *Why is she wishing me good morning in the middle of the afternoon?*

Her next words jolted me into reality. "We want you and your wife to appear on *Good Morning America* tomorrow morning. Can you be on a plane for New York in two hours?"

All at once the lights came on. I turned to my wife and asked, "Honey, can you be packed and ready to leave for New York in half an hour? They want us to appear on *Good Morning America*." Diane looked at me as though I had lost my mind—again. But thirty-two minutes later we were roaring down the freeway to the Portland airport. Unbelievable!

A sense of the miraculous hung in the air as we boarded the plane. We had watched the hand of God take one simple midweek service and broadcast it around the nation. It began when Diane and I decided to address an issue the church wasn't really talking about—at least not in a healthy way. We decided to take on the subject of the fun, joy, delight, and deep intimacy Christian couples can uniquely experience in their sexual relationship.

A local television station learned of our plans. I remember the female reporter who showed up before the Wednesday service. She asked me where she could find the Sexy Christians class. I'm sure she expected to locate the group lurking in a dark room where we could conceal everyone's identity. She was going to get the scoop on this nefarious activity.

I smiled and told her, "It's not a class. It's the subject of our midweek services for the entire month."

Her eyes dilated; her brows raised. She blurted out, "So what are you going to talk about?"

"Oh, lots of things. For example, tonight we'll put up pictures of the male and female sexual response cycles on our giant video screens."

Now her expression displayed even greater shock. She almost shouted her next question: "You're going to show pornography in the church?"

"No. No!" I hadn't meant to confuse her. "But it's definitely going to be a PG-13 service."

"What do you mean? What are you going to talk about?"

I smiled once again. I had to tease her a bit more. "Well, you'll just have to stick around and enjoy what happens."

A preservice meeting interrupted our discussion. I thanked my new friend for coming and asking such great questions. I assumed she and her team—like most news crews that visit one of our services—would disappear and I would never see them again. But they stayed for the entire service. The reporter busily took notes, and her crew filmed almost everything that happened.

This is unusual, I thought to myself. That was an understatement. The report appeared on the local evening news at ten o'clock and again at eleven. It aired again on the early morning news the following day. Next, CNN picked up the story and broadcast it around the nation and to several foreign countries. They posted it on their website, where it became one of the top video clips of the week.

If ever I have seen the hand of God take something and use it in a surprising way, it was that Wednesday night service. Since that first evening, Diane and I have led numerous Sexy Christians Seminars throughout our nation and around the world. The response has never changed. Our listeners display deep interest and profound longing for the things only God can give. And this is especially true for folks who don't normally go to church.

We arrived in New York around midnight, got a few hours of sleep, and appeared on the show the next morning. We received a welcome that would characterize our experience anytime we shared about Sexy Christians. The secular world was fascinated with what we had to say. First of all, these people found the term *Sexy Christians* an oxymoron. Their perception of Christians with respect to sexuality was extremely negative. They saw church folks as falling into one of two categories:

1. I call the first category "uptight and out of sight." These believers never talk about sex because they consider it dirty. They might not come right out and use the word, but you'd have to be blind, deaf, and dumb to not draw that conclusion. The tightly pursed lips say it all.
2. The secular world sees the other type of believer in an even more negative light. This is someone who preaches against sexual sin but has a secret life riddled with im-

morality. You can fill in the name of the latest fallen spiritual leader.

And yet as Diane and I shared our ideas with the television audience, you could sense the profound interest. The magnificent, elegant Robin Roberts interviewed us. With each of her questions, the people around the set leaned forward, intrigued by the dialogue. We walked away more convinced than ever that our world desperately needs to hear this message: Christ died for our sins and hang-ups so we might experience everything our Father God has for us. And that definitely includes being Sexy Christians!

After the interview, we walked out onto Times Square and suddenly I got it. I began to grasp what God was up to and why he had suddenly catapulted us into such visibility. As we stood there, the wind swirling around us, we found ourselves surrounded by an incredible surge of frenetic activity. Taxi horns blared incessantly. The thundering cacophony of construction sites assaulted our ears. The sheer volume of life in the Big Apple seemed overwhelming.

I looked up. In nearly every direction was a two- or three-story idol. These were not bronze or golden images of local gods but high-tech, huge plasma screens or otherwise exquisitely vivid pictures of seminude women. You couldn't escape them.

Tears came to my eyes. As we walked out of the studio, the crowd on the street corner had spontaneously applauded us. The crew of *Good Morning America* asked if they thought talking about sex in church was a good idea. "Yes!" came their overwhelming response.

I could now see why they responded so positively. The idols they saw all around them were promising fulfillment but leaving them empty. In the deepest part of their souls, they longed for the kind of intimacy Diane and I described. They longed to be Sexy Christians.

The Purpose

God's Design for Sexual and Spiritual
Fulfillment Encompasses His Basic
Purposes for Us as His Creation

1

Sexy Christians: An Oxymoron?

Can Christians Really Be Sexy?

TED

The brilliant, streaming rush of surface-to-air missiles. The ominous barrage of antiaircraft fire. As a Marine fighter pilot, I spent nearly a year flying over war-torn Vietnam, dodging flak and insanity. I had become used to sights and sounds like these, that is, until God abruptly pulled me into a conflict that I realized was even more vicious.

I had always pictured myself flying for the rest of my life. But God had another idea. As I like to put it, "I got drafted into the pastorate." After a brief stint in theological graduate school, I became immersed in an entirely new level of warfare. Now, instead of twisting and turning through a flak-filled sky, I found myself wrestling in prayer over the lives of the couples and singles who poured into my office.

Their stories all sounded the same. They were in trouble—deep trouble—in their relationships and their sexual lives. These were decent folks. They went to church, prayed, and read the latest books on marriage and relationships. But nothing seemed to work. That's why they kept showing up at my door.

Without exception their understanding of real intimacy and of their own sexuality was either nonexistent or deeply flawed. Somewhere in the counseling process I noticed that even the couples who were active in church and not at odds with one another had sex lives that were, at best, unfulfilling.

Somewhere in the counseling process I noticed that even the couples who were active in church and not at odds with one another had sex lives that were, at best, unfulfilling.

That's where this book began—deep in the battle of prayer and counseling these people who seemed so normal but had such deep-seated problems. One day as I looked at my counseling calendar, it all came into focus. An older couple was scheduled to meet with me. I had encountered them only briefly before, but they seemed like wonderful, outgoing, and gracious people. When I saw my secretary's note that they were coming in to discuss a marital issue, my first thought was one of disbelief: *What can I say to that kind of couple? They're twice my age with twice my experience level.*

At that point I made a wise choice. I acknowledged my limitations to God (I'm quite sure he already knew all about them) and asked for his assistance: *Lord, what would you have me say to these folks that would really help them?* Quietly and gently the Holy Spirit whispered one small sentence directly into my soul: *Ask the husband what he is holding against his wife.*

The couple arrived on time and greeted me cordially. I welcomed them, and we spent the first five minutes in small talk. We gravitated immediately to a safe topic for the Pacific Northwest: the weather (it seemed as though it had been raining for a month). We ventured on into another safe topic: the trials and tribulations of the University of Oregon football team.

As the surface discussion continued, I began to notice a weighty sense of sadness reflected in the wife's eyes. I knew the time had come for me to take the risk, to deliver the question the Holy Spirit had entrusted to me. I leaned toward the husband and asked abruptly, "Sir, do you have something you are holding against your wife?"

It was as though a jolt of electricity hit him smack in the center of his chest. "How did you know that?" he almost shouted back. Then, "You're darn right I do!" he continued sharply. "Ten years ago she had an affair with another man!" Tears welled up in his eyes. "And we have been fighting with each other ever since," he choked through the tears now streaming down his face.

Our conversation had taken an abrupt turn. As both husband and wife poured out their deep hurts and pain, my office began to fill with a sense of hopelessness. They had visited numerous counselors. Their sex life was nonexistent. Despite the fact that they were deeply committed to God and to their marriage, they were growing to dislike each other more each day.

At this point God moved me to be vulnerable and tell them simply, "I don't know how to mend your relationship. Sure, I've taken plenty of counseling classes and I have the academic degrees. But you've already heard most of what I intended to tell you. And sir, I sense you are struggling with sexual issues of your own. As a couple, you have literally wasted ten years of your marriage—ten years of sexual fulfillment and intimacy God had planned for you. Why don't we just get down on our knees together and sincerely ask him for help?"

"But she committed adultery!" the husband blurted.

I was already flying full throttle, so I continued on course. "Let me get this straight. The two of you have been living in hell for ten years because of something your wife did in the past—something you refuse to let go of? Is this true?"

"I guess so, now that you put it that way," he replied reluctantly.

I repeated my challenge: "Why don't we get down on our knees together and ask God for help?"

Some counseling scenes stick with you forever. Those soul-burning moments occur when the crushing defeat Satan has planned for a couple or an individual is completely blown away—the times when God's presence and glory explode through the problem. Slowly, the husband knelt beside his wife and began to pray, warring through his broken heart to the freedom God had offered all along. He grappled tremendously against his pain. At one point his face changed and I could almost see the spiritual version of a ceramic mask enfolding his features. As he wept and prayed, that mask seemed to crack and fall away. Suddenly he broke, collapsing into the arms of his weeping wife.

That's when things really began to get interesting. He looked up at me through a flood of tears, stammering, "I have wasted so many years!" By this time I was crying like a baby myself. I choked out, "Yes, that's true. But God can restore all the years the locust have eaten" (see Joel 1:4).

Almost immediately the couple began making up for lost time and seriously kissing. I backed up and headed for the door, mumbling awkwardly, "Hey, I'm leaving now, heading home to see my wife. After you guys are through, lock the door, would you?"

Can We Talk?

This couple was a classic picture of the fact that intimacy is not *being close and comfortable*. This is one of the great myths being taught in the world (even the Christian world) today. Intimacy is not *learning the latest sexual technique or fad* either. According to what we see in Scripture, true biblical intimacy is *developing the ability to be uncomfortably close and vulnerable with another imperfect human.* This may seem like an extreme statement until we realize the difficulty of true intimacy with Christ. His words point to the challenges of an intimate relationship with him:

> If anyone would come after me, he must deny himself and take up his cross daily and follow me.
>
> Luke 9:23

> Whoever finds his life will lose it, and whoever loses his life for my sake will find it.
>
> Matthew 10:39

Here's the critical point: *ultimately, the way we relate to Christ mirrors the way we relate to our spouse.* Paul made this clear when he instructed husbands to "love your wives, just as Christ loved the church and gave himself up for her" (Eph. 5:25). For some reason we have a hard time connecting the dots. We tend to see intimacy through the distorted lens of romantic fantasy rather than as one of the greatest spiritual growth tools God ever designed.

True biblical intimacy is developing the ability to be uncomfortably close and vulnerable with another imperfect human.

Only the grace of God can pull off something this impossible. That's why I tell people that Christians have a unique advantage when it comes to having a great sex life. *Sexy Christians* is not an oxymoron but an accurate description of the unique potential that followers of Christ have in their marital relationships. The tragedy is that so few couples understand

21

this fact, and even fewer understand how to put biblical intimacy into practice.

In this book, my wife and I hope to lead you on a great adventure—one we've been pursuing for more than forty years. We will help you discover your incredible sexual potential as a person who loves God. If you are still investigating the claims of Christ, this book is for you as well. In the depths of your sexuality, you will discern the hand of God in your life in ways you've probably never imagined.

Perhaps you've never read anything like that before this moment. It is the gospel truth. You see, God invented sex, and he knows it's one of his greatest gifts. This is why Satan finds such demented glee in twisting and distorting this area of our lives.

When Diane and I travel by plane to lead a seminar, a fascinating event occurs nearly every time. I strike up a conversation with the person seated next to me, and he or she asks me what I do. I reply that my wife and I will be presenting a Sexy Christians Seminar.

Not once have I ever received a negative response from someone who doesn't attend church. In fact, these people frequently make comments like, "You know, I might even go to church to hear a seminar like that."

Conversely, I find it absolutely amazing that the few negative responses we have received tend to come from Christians. At one church where we were scheduled to speak, the pastor received an irate phone call prior to our arrival. "Pastor, we shouldn't talk about things like this in the church!" the woman on the other end of the line declared emphatically.

"You mean sex?" he asked.

"Yes," she replied. "It just isn't appropriate."

"Well, are you saying sex is dirty, ma'am?"

"Well, no, Pastor, . . . but we shouldn't talk about it," she stammered.

How sad, I thought when the pastor relayed this conversation. Still, I understand the woman's hesitancy. Through our Sexy Christians Seminars, Diane and I have had the opportunity to ask thousands of believers, "How many of you had a mom or dad who talked to you in depth about sex as you grew up?"

The affirmative response rate is only 1 to 2 percent. Instead, most of us grew up hearing strange messages with dual implications like, "Sex is dirty; save it for someone you love."

This explains why we usually start a seminar by asking, "How about allowing us to take the role of your surrogate mom and dad in the faith? Over the next two days we will share with you the lessons God has taught us about having a dynamite marriage—sexually and spiritually."

The Missing Piece

As believers, we absolutely must have a framework to help us examine our marriage and our world. I say that so firmly because merely telling followers of Christ that sexual immorality is wrong doesn't work. It sure hasn't worked so far. Instead, we must give believers a clear vision of the God-given gift of their sexuality as followers of Christ.

Again, Christians have a distinctive advantage over non-Christians when it comes to sexual fulfillment. We'll prove this to you in the pages that follow. As believers, we need a clear vision of God's best for us if we intend to walk in purity. I define *vision* as "a vivid picture of what can be, motivated by a driving passion that it should be." The underlying problem: most Christians don't even remotely understand the truth of their potential as sexual beings.

Let's stop right here for a moment. I've worked with people long enough to know that some of you are thinking right now, *Wait just a minute, Ted. How can you say that it doesn't work to simply tell followers of Christ that sexual immorality is wrong and then turn around and declare that most Christians don't remotely understand the truth of their potential as sexual beings? Talk about sweeping generalizations. Come on, Ted. You can do better than that!*

Like all generalizations, these statements don't apply in every situation. In the majority of cases, however, I've found them to be sadly and precisely true. A recent study by comScore that measures internet traffic revealed that 66 percent of internet-using men in America between the ages of eighteen and thirty-four look at online porn at least once a month.[1] This finding has rather sobering implications with respect to the guy in the pew. Since the average amount of time spent cruising pornographic sites is two to four hours per visit, our guy in the pew is probably getting more porn per month than he is the Word of God.

In speaking at various men's conferences over the last decade, I have discovered the vast majority of men in the church are losing the battle for sexual purity. In two large men's conferences where I spoke recently, I asked the pastors if I could ask their men some honest questions. They granted permission, and over 90 percent of the attendees admitted they were struggling—and falling. In other words, the enemy has made dangerous inroads into the lives of many, including a number of our trusted leaders. Even more shocking is the fact that these were strong, healthy churches. At first the pastors were stunned, but now we are helping them get ministries in place to help these men experience real healing.

And men are not the only ones who have this problem. Online porn use is a systems problem that reaches every corner of the family. A recent study showed 40 percent of female internet users now engage in problematic cybersex behavior.[2] An even more troubling statistic reveals that twelve- to seventeen-year-olds have now become the largest consumers of internet pornography.[3]

Pastors are not immune to this struggle; in fact I believe they are particularly vulnerable. In the final chapter of this book I will share the shocking results of a recent clinical evaluation I did on evangelical pastors. My findings have shown such a dramatic problem that I have limited the clinical side of my ministry to pastors and other Christian leaders who are struggling sexually or who have experienced moral failure.

These troubling statistics help us understand that being a Sexy Christian is not the latest fad in self-fulfillment. It's not a catchy phrase to advertise a sermon series. And the book you're reading right now is not simply another entry in a long line of self-help books designed to spruce up your sex life.

Diane and I are writing this book because we believe something is missing. No matter how much we pray, develop tremendous worship experiences, or design new evangelism and church growth programs, the issue of deep hurt in the sexual arena continues to eat at the heart of the church. Something's missing, and we want to help individuals, families, and churches find and fill the gap.

The problems run rampant not only in America but around the world. As we work on this manuscript, Diane and I have just returned from a ministry trip to the Netherlands and Central America. Throughout Central America we had the joy of sharing Sexy Christians Seminars. Sex is a universal language, and sexual struggles are a universal problem. The picture of couples coming forward at the end of the seminar with tears streaming down their faces will remain with me until I see the Lord. It is a picture of men and women, including church staff members with whom I met one-on-one, all weeping because they had thought there was no hope, no way out of the sexual bondage they had battled for years.

Of course there is hope. Jesus Christ has conquered the grave and hell. The devil is a liar.

The denomination we met with in the Netherlands—a country known around the world for its sexual immorality—has decided to take on the monster of sexual bondage. These churches refuse to lose the next generation to this horrific battle. Instead, they intend to begin dealing with sexual addiction in an open and gracious manner. They will start by providing small groups in which people can find real help with their struggles without being shamed or told, "Just stop it. Pray. You have a willpower problem." They have come to realize this is one of the key battles for the church in the twenty-first century.

I am sure you can think of numerous other issues today's church needs to address, but none is more critical. Why? In the Old Testament, before God led Israel into the Promised Land, he made a striking declaration: "So do not act like the people in Egypt, where you used to live, or like the people of Canaan, where I am taking you. You must not imitate their way of life" (Lev. 18:3 NLT).

As the passage continues, God identifies the types of behavior he finds particularly offensive. This section of Scripture reads like the front page of your local newspaper, listing one sexual sin after another in graphic detail. Finally, he records the ultimate cost of engaging in such behavior: "For all these things were done by the people who lived in the land before you, and the land became defiled. And if you defile the land, it will vomit you out as it vomited out the nations that were before you" (Lev. 18:27–28).

I bet you know the story. In many ways, the Old Testament reminds me of a slow-motion video replay of an aircraft accident (something I had to watch often as a military safety officer). The prophets cried out for the nation of Israel to pull up from her impending crash. From Amos to Hosea, from Isaiah to Jeremiah, they warned of the folly of worshipping the gods of the surrounding nations. The Israelites' syncretistic brand of worship in these lands included enough sexual perversion to fill a XXX porn site.

And what happened after the prophets' dire warnings? Israel ignored God again and again. The consequences were devastating, the crash catastrophic.

The Rest of the Story

The same thing could happen to our nation and our world. But what if we write a different ending for the story—an unexpected ending like the one God wrote for the older couple who came into my office that memorable day? They had wasted ten years in strife, guilt, and misery when God used the tool of biblical intimacy to begin releasing them into the wholeness and healing he had planned all along. As they spent time working through the Scriptures and participated in our marriage ministry, God did amazing things to restore their relationship.

Rather than hiding their pain from the world around them and wearing masks to cover the brokenness inside, they allowed God to reveal his glory in their lives through the *missing piece* of biblical intimacy. He used their weakness as a tool for his strength. As they came to know him more deeply, they grew even more in love with each other. As he often does, God chose to use their years of struggle to encourage others, and they became vibrant marriage mentors within our church body.

Thank God this couple had the courage to experience the truth of Paul's magnificent declaration: "Whoever is a believer in Christ is a new creation. The old way of living has disappeared. A new way of living has come into existence" (2 Cor. 5:17 GW). This allowed them to stop the chronic pain of identifying themselves only according to their past wounds. Instead, as they held on to Jesus and one another, they came to a glorious realization of Christ's present-tense love for them. They caught his vision for the fulfilling future he intended for their lives and their marriage. They became Sexy Christians.

When Christian couples begin to move from their brokenness into discovering and experiencing the full beauty of what God has for them sexually, it will truly change our world. Those couples will shine like beacons in a world of spiritual darkness. Their purpose, power, and passion will be contagious. As Diane and I keep saying, "We want to start a sexual revolution of the heavenly kind."

Below are some comments from those who are seeing this in their own lives and homes through the truths of our Sexy Christians Seminars. They have joined the revolution.

> "It helped me learn more about my wife in one night than I normally would have over several months, through inspiring conversation with her."

> "This is the most important seminar for your marriage *ever*."

> "It's the answer to the best sex you'll ever have—throw away the *Cosmopolitan* magazines!"

> "It helped me understand my wife in a healthy way and treat her with respect."

> "It's very enlightening; it will help you deal with any issue you might have regarding intimacy. It is the best seminar on sex I've attended."

> "Every marriage needs to experience this seminar. It is real, refreshing, and restorative. I have never seen anything like it. I believe this will save many marriages from disaster. It is the only seminar of its kind—extremely healing and effective."

> "Do you want to light the flame in your marriage? This seminar will strengthen a strong marriage and bring healing to a struggling one."

Don't settle for a *good* relationship and sex life when God intends his incredible gift of biblical intimacy to be nothing less than *great*!

In the pages ahead you will discover that your sexuality and spirituality are profoundly intertwined. That's why we want to challenge you to rev up your sex life and your spiritual life. After every chapter, we will present "Love Lessons" that summarize our teaching and help you tie these two areas together. Instead of homework, we will give you some very personal, practical, and fun "Home Play" exercises to assist you in growing together with your spouse both sexually and spiritually.

You see, this isn't the kind of book that allows you merely to read the concepts and walk away changed. If you genuinely want to experience all God intends for your relationship, you must put the truths into practice. When you do, I guarantee you: this book will change your life.

Finally, you may be reading *Sexy Christians* as a person who doesn't attend church. Maybe someone gave it to you as a gift. Please don't let the references I make to spirituality scare you away. Your marriage deserves the very best. You obviously care about it or you wouldn't be reading this book. I want to make the same promise to you as well: this

Don't settle for a good relationship and sex life when God intends his incredible gift of biblical intimacy to be nothing less than great!

book will change your life. God cares for you deeply. If you follow his pathway for relationships, he will graciously touch your life. He will faithfully pour out his richest blessings upon you and your mate.

Get ready for an entirely new relationship. Get ready to become a Sexy Christian.

Love Lessons

God wants you to have an incredible sex life.

God created the sexual relationship as an expression of his love—a beautiful, intimate picture of all he intends us to be. Satan has entered the picture to twist what God pronounced good, leaving people trapped in sexual bondage and addiction. In *Sexy Christians*, we hope to begin a sexual revolution of the very best kind, moving people to the healing and health that will cause them to shine as lights in a world of darkness. As you work through each chapter and put its principles into practice, God will use this book to change your life.

Home Play

Every game has its ground rules, and Home Play is no different. Use these to keep the playing field level when you respond to your spouse: (1) Avoid "you" statements. Instead, talk about your own actions, thoughts, and feelings. (2) Listen. Don't give advice or attempt to psychoanalyze your spouse. (3) If tempers flare, disengage and pray.

1. Take time to reflect on the title of this book. Circle the answer that best describes the first thing that came to mind when you saw it.

    a. What on earth is a "Sexy Christian"?
    b. Oh no, another book about wrapping yourself in plastic wrap or painting each other's toenails.
    c. What a great idea!
    d. I don't know what that is, but it definitely sounds interesting.

2. The authors define biblical intimacy as "being uncomfortably close and vulnerable with another imperfect human." Can you name a couple who you believe practices biblical intimacy? If so, discuss the things you admire about their relationship.

3. Do you agree that "Christians have a unique advantage when it comes to having a great sex life" (page 21)? Why or why not?

4. In the story that opens this chapter, Ted describes the way God used a pointed question and a time of prayer to help restore a broken marriage. Take this opportunity to pray with your spouse, if possible, about your study of this material. The prayer can be as simple and short as you like. Just take turns speaking to God from your heart. Then watch to see what he does.

2

The Magic of the Moment

How Do I Know I Married the Right Person?

TED

Heads swiveled as her heels clicked smartly down the long hall of the engineering building. Jet-black hair and a fluorescent Hawaiian dress accentuated a surfer girl tan. Combined, they left almost the entire nuclear physics wing gawking in her wake. As the mystery woman passed a group of students loitering outside a classroom, her gorgeous head turned ever so slightly to one side. "Hi!" came her bright, confident voice. Clearly, all systems were up and running, all operations complete. Her pace never faltered as she continued her course and disappeared through the glass doors at the hallway's end.

Stunned to an abrupt halt in my normal Monday morning rush, I found my mind filled with questions instead of its normal jumble of math and astrophysics problems. *Who is she? Why is she here? What is a woman (an incredibly beautiful one) doing in the engineering building anyway?* Feet firmly planted, I craned my neck to stare after her retreating footsteps. My gaze swept the hallway from side to side. *Please let her come back. Please let her see me. Please!*

Back for the same class at the same time that Wednesday morning, I was in full scanning mode, all radar on high alert. *Will she return? What will she say?* There she was, dead ahead! An awkward "Hi" croaked its way from my throat, met almost instantly by the second silky-smooth greeting of the week. As quickly as she had reappeared, however, she was gone, gliding regally down the hallway while still more heads turned in wonder. *I can't believe it; she actually showed up again! Now, how am I gonna find out her number? Would a dream girl like that ever consider going out with me?*

You guessed it. Diane was the gorgeous mystery woman, and our initial hallway encounters soon grew into much more. Some swift but serious investigation yielded her name and number. I made the call despite sweaty palms and a trembling voice. She followed my halting offer—"Would you like to go out sometime?"—with a long and terrifying pause.

Years later the engine of a fighter aircraft quit on me in midair. That silence was nowhere near as horrific as the one I experienced over the phone as I waited for Diane's reply. Finally, amazingly, the beautiful object of my desire responded with a simple, "Sure, I'd love to."

Gone Fishing

I'm glad our story doesn't end there. What I didn't know (until nearly two years and one wedding later) was that it hadn't begun with a chance hallway encounter. I wasn't the initial pursuer after all. My conniving bride-to-be had seen me in the library, made a positive assessment, and deliberately set her bait. A primary education major would not typically travel through the engineering building. Diane was—as she remains today—a woman with a plan. Her seemingly random walk down the hall was actually a carefully orchestrated fishing trip. And every day I'm thankful I swallowed the hook.

My future wife's fishing expedition would change the course of both our lives forever. A number of things combined to produce the magic of the moment, a unique piece of shared history we love to recall to this day. When she and I first met in the engineering hallway, we could never have foreseen the long years of love and intimacy stretching ahead. We could not have anticipated our two children and four grandchildren or our God-called partnership in ministry and marriage. And neither of us could have foreseen the commitment to Christ that changed our lives much more than our first meeting.

Ultimately Diane's faith commitment led to my own. It happened during my military service in Vietnam on a day when I had faced one of the worst challenges of my life: killing several men at close range. My best effort to numb the raging pain was to drink myself into an alcoholic stupor. That night, as I lay half drunk in a lonely bunker, I received a care package sent by my bride. The letter Diane enclosed with the package met my need much more directly than the mugs of beer I had consumed so eagerly. Her words spoke tenderly of her love for me and for her Lord, touching me to the wounded core of my being. As a rocket attack sounded overhead, I knelt to make my peace: "I have always believed in you, God. I don't know who this Jesus Christ is, but sign me up."

"It's All Coming Back to Me Now"

Diane and I love to ask couples about the magic of the moment when they first met because we love hearing about the creative ways God brings people together. Through the years, we've learned that something special happens when husbands and wives—even those having a hard time making their marriage work—share their stories. In nearly every case, their eyes soften and their voices warm as they express the magic of their first hours together.

Celine Dion's great song "It's All Coming Back to Me Now" eloquently expresses the same magic. It opens with the wrenching pain of a couple who have hurt one another deeply. Quickly, the song moves into the haunting refrain, sung as only Celine can: "But when you touch me like this, and you hold me like that, I just have to admit that it's all coming back to me."[1]

Why did this song become so popular? Because it touches a place deep in the heart of everyone who hears it. It pierces past the daily traffic of our reasoning processes to the depths of our souls, down to what neuroscientists call the limbic system[2] and what Scripture calls our "heart" (our will, fundamental thoughts, and emotions).[3] Here in the limbic system we develop foundational response patterns designed to help us avoid pain. The limbic system also records pleasurable, rewarding experiences and creates deep mental pathways to repeat them. After more than two decades of counseling individuals who struggle with sexual issues, I've discovered a vital truth: *when faith overcomes fear, bondage can be defeated.*

When faith overcomes fear, bondage can be defeated.

The process works like this: First, the marriage partners learn to trust God again as they face their inner struggles. In order for this to occur, they must deal with the avoidance patterns deep within their hearts. Typically they have used these false paths to medicate the hurts of life since their childhood or early teen years, so these ruts run deep. Yet the grace of God is far more powerful than anything the enemy could ever devise.

Second, the couple must learn to trust not only God but other people as well. Since almost all of our deep wounds are created within the context of human relationships, our healing comes in relationships as well. We can't change or find restoration in a vacuum.

I can always recognize the moment in counseling when a couple has reached a true breakthrough. It happens when they turn toward one another and rediscover the magic of the moment that first drew them together. I've seen the power of that moment again and again. In fact, research shows original feelings between spouses change very little over time.[4] Of course every couple faces ups and downs. Feelings can diminish, especially when circumstances have led to a drifting apart. But couples who take time to mentally revisit the events that brought them together—the magic of their own unique moment—will find that although the associated feelings may lie dormant, they remain inside waiting to be revived and rediscovered.

After watching this sequence of events recur with couple after couple, counseling session after counseling session, I'm convinced that *the Holy Spirit uniquely blesses those who deliberately choose to remember the magic of that God-ordained moment.* The reward pathways God plants deep in our hearts are far stronger than any rabbit trails of destruction or cul-de-sac of curse the enemy uses to distract us. So remember the magic of the moment and rejoice in God's good work in your lives.

Divine Encounters

Why does the Holy Spirit anoint those moments so beautifully? I see a clear reason: you and your spouse did not meet by accident. A sovereign, passionate, and romantic God was at work in your lives long before you first noticed one another. I love the way Paul expresses this dazzling truth: "Long before he laid down earth's foundations, he had us in mind, had settled on us as the focus of his love, to be made whole and holy by his love" (Eph. 1:4 Message).

Read this statement again; let it sink into your soul. Do you somehow think God chose only *you*? Paul is emphatic: God chose *us*. Call me a ridiculous romantic, a heretic, whatever. Each of us has free will, but God, in the mystery of his sovereignty, brought you and your spouse together. When a couple truly realizes this fact, it changes everything.

This same truth, however, can generate a tremendous amount of anxiety for a single person. Without deep study and understanding, it can lead to concerns like, "What if I get it wrong and mess up God's choice for me?" Singles who love Christ often ask me this question. I always smile and ask them a couple of questions in return. "Are you trying to walk with Christ?"

"Yes, Pastor, with all my heart."

"Are you purposefully living in any known sin?"

"No. Sure, I mess up every now and then, but I don't purposely ignore God."

At that point I usually chuckle and drop a theological bomb. "Then you can't miss it or mess it up. You serve a sovereign God who is outrageously in love with you. If you ever get concerned about his radical love, look at the valentine of the cross. I guarantee that at the right time, if Jesus has called you to marry, he will bring someone into your life who loves him deeply and who will also ring your bell."

Allow me to confess something right now. Years ago, even after I came to know Christ, I would have considered such a statement ludicrous. Most likely I would have responded with something like, "That's crazy. I'm the one who chose Diane to be my wife. Why, I didn't even believe in God at the time."

Marriage (especially more than forty years of it) does at least one thing for you. You come to realize that most of the time *you didn't have a clue.*

My point in sharing all this is to make it clear that your spouse is a gift from God. You didn't meet by accident. If you have said yes to Christ, you serve an omniscient and awesome God. He was at work in your life long before you were conscious of his touch. And even if you don't consider yourself one of his followers, he remains at work all around you, preparing circumstances and situations designed to draw you closer to him.

"But Ted, we met in a bar," or, "We lived together before we got married," and so on. It doesn't matter. Was there sin in the early stages of your relationship? Then get down on your knees together and ask God for forgiveness. Dust the crud off the past. Refuse to allow it to abort the sovereign purposes of God in your life.

Don't live a moment longer with anything less than the wonderful plans God has for you. Even if you two drive each other nuts, you share a God-ordained magic. Drive a stake of his grace solidly in the ground and rediscover the magic of the moment—that sovereign moment when you met—that outrageous moment when the sparks flew and heaven rejoiced—that beautiful moment when human passion was mysteriously touched by divine potential.

Action Plan

Some might say Diane's approach in the engineering hallway that day was unbiblical. You need to understand: although Diane is a born-again believer, she is also Jewish. As she planned her fishing expedition, she was unknowingly following a time-honored Old Testament pattern. Have you heard the story of Ruth and Boaz? Ruth finds herself single because her husband died. After a time of mourning and a move, her mother-in-law, Naomi, gives her some great advice:

> Boaz is a close relative of ours, and he's been very kind by letting you gather grain with his workers. Tonight he will

be winnowing barley at the threshing floor. Now do as I tell
you—take a bath and put on perfume and dress in your nicest
clothes. Then go to the threshing floor, but don't let Boaz see
you until he has finished his meal.

Ruth 3:2–3 NLT

Basically, what Naomi is saying is, "Listen, girl. Put on
some of that Moabite perfume. You know, the Moabite Mon-
key Business. Get on your red dress and high heels. Have your
teeth whitened. Get your hair done. Hit the tanning booth
and put on your best makeup. So far, this guy has only seen
you in the field covered with sweat, your hair up in a rag."

"But Ted, a woman shouldn't chase a man," you may say.
Maybe not, but you sure can get his attention. Most men tend
to be less than bright when it comes to things like this. They
can find themselves rushing to a class and not even realize
who or what is coming their way.

Naomi's advice is filled with wisdom. She doesn't tell Ruth
to come up to Boaz and start pleading her case. She advises
against publicly demanding to know if the relationship is
headed anywhere. Wisely, she tells Ruth to wait until the man
has had his fill of Big Macs, hung out with the guys, and
watched the game on the plasma screen television. Then—and
only then—should you (like Ruth) make your approach.

But when you do, don't hold back. Be bold in your pursuit
of God's purpose in your life. This is not about hustling a
man. It is about hungering after God's best. If the guy fails to
respond, no big deal. It simply means he is not the one God
has for you. It doesn't mean you are a loser. Instead, you are
a *chooser*—a person who passionately chooses to trust God
to meet the deepest needs of your heart.

One of the truly delightful lessons taught in Scripture explains how to free a godly woman to be herself. We find the
classic example of this in another Old Testament book, the
Song of Songs. Also referred to as the Song of Solomon,
its Hebrew designation as the Song of Songs reveals that

God considers this the greatest love song ever written. We know this because the Hebrew language contains a superlative structure quite different from English constructions. In Hebrew, when you want to say something is the very best, you don't change the form of the word. Instead, you repeat it. That's why we call Christ the *King of kings* and *Lord of lords*. Those are Hebraic expressions. So by calling this tiny book of the Old Testament the Song of Songs, God defines it as the greatest love song of all time. And I'd love to hear Celine sing it!

Love Story

The setting: Israel, tenth century BC. King Solomon, the most eligible bachelor on the planet, travels to the northern part of his kingdom. During the business trip he falls head over heels in love with the farmer's daughter, Shulamith. It's an incredible story. In the book's eight short chapters, we get to listen in on their courtship, their honeymoon night, and even their conflicts. In the 117 verses found in the book, Shulamith is speaking approximately 60 percent of the time. And she is not just talking; she is usually telling Solomon what she desires sexually. Notice the following examples:

> Let him kiss me with the kisses of his mouth—for your love is more delightful than wine.
>
> Song of Songs 1:2

> My lover is to me a sachet of myrrh resting between my breasts.
>
> Song of Songs 1:13

> His left arm is under my head, and his right arm embraces me.
>
> Song of Songs 2:6

She says all this before they are even married! Shulamith is telling her fiancé in detail how she looks forward to being loved by him. This woman is every husband's dream: deeply virtuous but also outgoing, confident, and sexually free. She looks forward to experiencing all kinds of creative sexual activities with her husband alone. In fact, I'd call her the original Sexy Christian wife.

Not long before I left the pastorate to work full-time with Pure Desire Ministries International (PDMI), I led our flock through a study of the Song of Songs. I had done this several other times in the more than twenty years I served as senior pastor of East Hill Church. This time, though, something was different; it was definitely PG-13. The women in the congregation clearly came to appreciate Shulamith's style and freedom, which is why I had to warn them: "If you're engaged, please don't start talking to your fiancé as Shulamith did unless you're within a few weeks of being married. Otherwise we'll end up with a bunch of guys taking cold showers all night. And in Oregon, they might freeze to death. You could lose your man before you even get started."

> *[Shulamith] is every husband's dream: deeply virtuous but also outgoing, confident, and sexually free.*

In the chapters ahead we are going to talk about the Song of Songs you can experience in your life. God longs for you to encounter real intimacy to the depths of your being. You were made for connectedness; in fact, you will die without it. Perhaps you won't face immediate physical death, but a life without intimacy spells emotional death and destruction. The phrase *real intimacy* refers to the fact that intimacy is a multidimensional reality. It reaches beyond mere physical experience to the emotional and relational realms.

Scripture (in the Song of Songs and elsewhere) reveals the profound insight that all three dimensions of intimacy are deeply interconnected as displayed in the context of a relationship with the Lord. We see frequent encouragements in Scripture to dance and clap our hands before him (Pss. 47:1; 149:3). Intimacy with God is obviously emotional as well. The Bible encourages us to express a full range of emotion in our walk with him (Luke 6:21; Rom. 12:15).

Part of what creates true intimacy is the mystery of the differences between us as men and women. We'll explore this in the next chapter. In the meantime, make sure to go over the Love Lessons and Home Play exercises that follow. You don't want to miss any truths God has for you, and you certainly don't want to deprive yourself or your partner of the intimacy for which he created you. Remember, you're learning to be a Sexy Christian. Go for it!

Love Lessons

Your spouse is a gift from God.

God chose the two of you together. He not only has a purpose for you to fulfill, but he also has one for the two of you to fulfill together. Learn to honor, as a couple, the moment you met. That significant meeting held a measure of heaven at work. A sovereign event occurred: heaven and earth kissed, and God smiled.

Honor this precious piece of eternity by telling your kids the story of how you met. Repeat it frequently. The magic of this moment should be part of your family's history of faith. Your kids are not an accident and neither is your marriage. Don't ever let Satan convince you otherwise. Once you fully grasp that truth, you'll view life differently, you'll view your spouse differently, and you'll also become an incredible threat to the forces of darkness. Never, never become casual about something as sovereign and precious as your partnership, and never let your sex life become an expression of habit. Like Shulamith, resolve to become a sexy believer,

Never become casual about something as sovereign and precious as your partnership, and never let your sex life become an expression of habit.

and then become a sexy couple. As you work through and beyond this book, strive to become a Sexy Christian who looks forward to a lifetime of loving intimacy.

Godly women can be passionate and sexually responsive.

The concept that a godly woman is sexually passive comes straight from the pit of hell. Wives, remember it's biblical to pursue God's best in every area of your life, including your sexuality. Husbands, consider it your privilege to help your wife experience new levels of sexual freedom and responsiveness. That happens when you meet her physical, emotional, and spiritual needs as only a husband can. The chapters ahead will lead us on a fascinating journey to discover how.

Home Play

Rules in review: (1) Avoid "you" statements. Instead, talk about your own actions, thoughts, and feelings. (2) Listen. Don't give advice or attempt to psychoanalyze your spouse. (3) If tempers flare, disengage and pray.

1. Do you agree with Ted's statement, "You and your spouse did not meet by accident"? Why or why not?

2. Draw a picture or write three phrases to describe the way you felt about your future spouse within the first few weeks of the magical moment when you first met.

3. On the following scale (1 low, 10 high) mark your own level of activity in pursuing intimacy with your spouse:

   1   2   3   4   5   6   7   8   9   10

4. Take time to remember the magic of the moment when you and your mate first met. Next, take turns telling each other what you recall. Pray together and thank God for this life-changing time.

3

Strangers and Aliens

Why Are the Two of Us So Different?

TED

It was a typical vacation shopping trip. Diane happily led me from one fluff 'n puff store to another. Such emporiums, awash in estrogen, contain an amazing variety of items guaranteed to add touches of delicate grace to your home. Over the years I've developed a practiced tolerance for these boutiques.

It probably won't surprise you to learn that I prefer showrooms filled with sports items. As you browse there you can almost smell the sweat, hear the crack of the bat, or savor the fine-tuned whine of a high-performance triathlon bike. I revel in emporiums of testosterone where the thunderous sounds of a packed stadium or the whir of a perfect fly cast seem to echo through the aisles. Today, however, I had no ball glove to pound, no bike to ride, no late-model fishing reel to examine. Instead I found myself staring at a collection of dried flowers and scented candles. Diane had landed at a particular corner of the store, and I, in another corner, had nearly reached the limits of my estrogen tolerance. I needed intervention, and fast. Almost immediately my eyes fell upon an old-fashioned kaleidoscope. Tucked among the dried flowers, it added an unexpected touch to the otherwise feminine display.

Finally, a guy toy. I picked up the instrument and began to turn its barrel, revealing ever-changing patterns of color and beauty. *What a relief*, I thought. *I can play with this device for as long as it takes Diane to finish browsing.*

Suddenly it happened. As I adjusted the kaleidoscope barrel, I observed its shifting colors with one eye and out of the other eye caught sight of Diane. Instantly I recognized the similarity. *Diane and the kaleidoscope—each a fascinating, ever-changing picture of beauty and color.*

What's the Difference?

Without Diane's delightful touch, my life would resemble the inside of a kaleidoscope without the reflective prisms: drab and dull. So how can the woman who brings me so much delight and vitality also frustrate me so much? Over the years I've learned the joys and the problems we experience in our marriage usually arise from the same fact: *we are so different.* Each of us has qualities that make us fundamentally, foundationally, radically different from one another.

Some recent primetime television specials explored the differences between men and women. I found these especially fascinating because the producers based their work on current research regarding the male and female brain. Dr. Lewis Judd, former director of the National Institute of Mental Health, summed up the revolution taking place in neurological research: "The pace of progress in neuroscience is so great that 90 percent of all we know about the brain we have learned in the last ten years."[1]

Based on this research, the television specials wrestled with questions like the following: Do women talk more than men? Do men listen less than women? Do men read maps better than women? The questions made for an interesting hour or two of television viewing, but the central truth of the research came through crystal clear: men and women have totally different brains. This fact has huge repercussions for our sexuality.

Men and women have totally different brains.

Years earlier the great theologian and aging sex goddess Raquel Welch said, "The mind can also be an erogenous zone."[2] Scientific studies of the brain now agree with her evaluation. Our brain, at about three pounds, is indeed the largest sex organ in our body. And in this case, size does matter. As we age, the brain can become less and less active. It can also decrease in overall mass. As it dims in activity over the decades, so too can our sexual function. The major reason for sexual and brain dysfunction is decreased blood flow.[3] When it comes to sexuality, the old adage proves true: use it or lose it.

Within only seventy-two hours of birth, marked differences in males and females can be seen. Females move their lips much more than males and focus more quickly on human faces. Males, in contrast, move their lips much less frequently and tend to focus on objects rather than human faces.[4]

Why do such visible differences exist? Research reveals that during the eighth week of pregnancy the embryonic male brain suddenly becomes radically different from the embryonic female brain, which occurs in conjunction with a flood of testosterone. This explains why the female brain has approximately 40 percent more connective tissue between right and left sides than the male brain.[5] It appears that testosterone unzips the male brain, and for the first two years after birth the male brain is awash in adult levels of testosterone that further cement these changes. As for females, adult levels of estrogen flood their brains for the first two years after birth. Dr. Louann Brizendine, author of the book *The Female Brain*, sums this up: "There is no unisex brain. Girls arrive already wired as girls, and boys arrive already wired as boys. Their brains are different by the time they're born."[6]

These differences deepen during adolescence when another hormone flood hits. As a result, the amygdala (an almond-shaped brain organ responsible for emotional memories and responses) of a teenage boy is twice as large as a teenage girl's. This explains why the average adolescent male thinks about sex every fifty-two seconds.[7] (I think my own average was every twenty-five seconds. I must have been hit by a hormonal tsunami.)

In teenage girls, on the other hand, the brain develops a stronger connection between the amygdala and the cerebral cortex (the higher reasoning and impulse control portion of the brain). This is why you never see teenage girls starring in MTV's *Jackass* series. Inside their brains, the cerebral cortex talks to and helps control the amygdala instead of allowing it to fire away randomly. This also explains why a teenage boy's brain lags about two years behind a girl's developmentally. Face it: it's hard to develop your brain when you're thinking about sex every fifty-two seconds. In adolescent girls the hippocampus (the emotional memory part of the brain) is blossoming, causing them to place a high priority on emotional and relational experiences. In fact, these mental developments remain in adulthood.[8] These facts help explain a behavior that mystified me for years—the phenomenon of the Potty Posse.

Different by Design

Never have I been tempted to recruit a Potty Posse when Diane and I have been out with other couples for dinner. Not once have I ever stood up and said to the fellow seated next to me, "Hey Frank, let's go to the bathroom together." Women, however, have this experience often. One decides it's time to go to the bathroom and the other ladies spontaneously join her. That's the power of the Potty Posse and of the differences between men and women.

You see, guys don't do things like that; it never enters our brains to respond that way. Sure, we have rules about using the bathroom that every male instinctively knows. When you're in the bathroom, you don't have deep, meaningful conversations with one another. You can grunt, scratch, or talk about the ball game. That's legal. But sharing your heart with another guy while you're there? That's weird. If it happens, it's time to turn around and get out of there fast. And by the way, that explains why there's almost never a line for the men's room. Guys, you know the drill: get in there, do your business, get out.

Researchers discovered what you already know. teen girls go off to the bathroom in packs and begin to talk freely with one another. Safe in the Potty Posse, they don't have to worry about either their parents or the boys overhearing them. During these conversations their brains experience a release of oxytocin and dopamine. Talking and hugging each other literally gives them a high.[9]

What may seem like a silly illustration underscores the radical differences between men and women. And because our brains are so different, our sexual response cycles are radi-

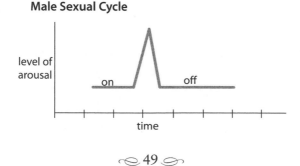

Male Sexual Cycle

cally different as well. Guys, I realize you've been wondering when I would get around to sex. We've arrived! On page 49 is a diagram of the typical male sexual response cycle.

The younger the guy, the steeper the peak and the shorter the time span. The best analogy of this response cycle is probably a light switch. On-Off; On-Off in a fairly rapid pattern.

As shown below, the female sexual response cycle is considerably more complex.

Female Sexual Cycle

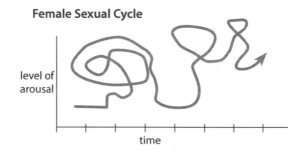

Of course this diagram assumes the woman's mental computer doesn't have multiple windows open and operating at the same time. Most women juggle a tangled mixture of thoughts and feelings simultaneously. And about half of them have stored thoughts and feelings from the past that regularly pop up into active mode whether they want them to or not.[10] Unlike men, they can't easily close those windows.

When I explain the female response cycle to a group of men, I like to use the analogy of an iron. "Gentlemen, you plug it in. Then you wait, and wait, and wait, and wait . . ." By the third repetition, most of the guys are smiling and nodding their heads.

This dash of humor helps me address what many people consider a delicate subject. Truthfully, most couples sense the huge gap in their sexual response cycles but have never discussed it. This means they've never understood how radically different they are, but the figure on page 51 makes it quite clear.

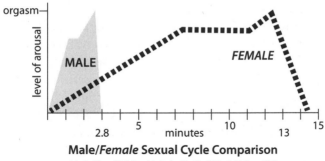

Male/*Female* Sexual Cycle Comparison
Adapted from "Relationship Rescue" by Dr. Phillip C. McGraw. PhD.

In our Sexy Christians Seminars, I let this diagram remain on the screen for a while before I ask, "Anyone notice the possibility of a problem here?" I then point out that the male response cycle lasts about two to three minutes while the female's lasts more than thirteen minutes—even without multiple windows open on her mental computer. This leaves at least a ten-minute gap between the two.

Then I point out, "Gentlemen, this gap is called 'foreplay.' And that doesn't mean shouting, 'Ready or not, here I come!'"

I'd like you to pause here for a moment. Add up all the astonishing differences between men and women. We have different brains, bodies, hormone surges, backgrounds, and perspectives. You can draw only one conclusion from all these incredible dissimilarities: *the frustrations and conflicts that seem to be so much a part of married life at times are all normal responses to God's divine design.* The differences between the two sexes have such deep roots in the physical, emotional, and spiritual aspects of our lives that the only way we can explain them is his creative power.

To Die For

Like our relationship with God, marriage comes with built-in challenges to self-centeredness. Into the fantasy world of our innocence and self-sufficiency, marriage explodes like a nuclear bomb. The moment we say *I do*, marriage declares an open war on our selfishness. Unfortunately, most husbands and wives don't realize that blaming and having to be right only lead to the graveyard of fools. After counseling couples for over twenty years in a variety of settings, I have decided that *marriage is one of God's most powerful tools to revolutionize and cleanse the human heart*. This explains why, as believers, our sexual relationship goes beyond the physical. It reaches down to the core and character of our hearts and souls.

The frustrations and conflicts that seem to be so much a part of married life at times are all normal responses to God's divine design.

I desperately try to communicate this truth during the premarital counseling process. But I can still have a hard time getting through to the average groom. Often I ask the eager young man, "What's the purpose of marriage?" Typically, he gets a testosterone-loaded look in his eyes and mumbles something like, "Woman."

That's when I lean over and confront him face-to-face. "Listen, son, the purpose of marriage is to crucify you." Normally this statement breaks through the fog of even the most unwitting groom. And when it does, he immediately asks for clarification. I point out that up until this phase in his life he has seen himself as rather unselfish. But once he gets married, his wife will provide a detailed list of just how self-centered he is.

"The killer," I tell the not-quite-as-eager groom, "is that she is usually right." Still, a prospective husband can have a hard time seeing this. As a single guy, he basically did what he wanted to do when he wanted to do it. It's time for me to inform him, "Those days are over, big boy. You'll have to move into a new phase or your sex life together will become dull and unfulfilling."

This final comment about their sex life usually closes the deal. Somewhat subdued, he says, "I get it," and agrees to pray with me. He has decided to put his wife first for more than just the ten-minute gap in their sexual response cycles.

Six months or so later I hear a troubled knock on my office door. There stands the young groom, disheveled and discouraged. "Pastor," he cries despondently, "my wife is killing me!"

Patiently I review the premarital briefings in which I pointed out he should expect this to occur. One young man responded to this review process by blurting out, "But *I'm* the head of the house!"

"Do you really know what being head of the house means?" I asked him. He didn't have a clue, so I helped him out. "In your home, you are like Christ, the head of the church. This means you are first to the cross. Welcome to marriage."

Light Show

God used the antique kaleidoscope to remind me of the changing beauty of the marriage between Diane and me. The barrel of the relationship kaleidoscope turns as the years go by. Even though we've now passed our fortieth anniversary, the Holy Spirit frequently jolts me into a new awareness of the gift we share. I see patterns and designs God has sovereignly created in us as husband and wife: opposites in so many areas that reflect his creative hand at work; differences that only grow stronger through the years; patterns of perception like shards of glass, each reflecting and refracting God's truth in unique forms and hues.

I'm sad to say that for about the first ten years of our marriage I was constantly trying to get Diane to agree with me. I wanted her to see the truth or, in this case, reality as I saw it. Over the years I've learned the "I'm right and you're wrong" view of life holds no beauty. After all, God is the only one with a total grasp on reality. And in his sovereign wisdom he brought us together as husband and wife to reflect his glory, not our own.

Our differences confront us with our need for God's grace as nothing else does. Understanding his grace toward us will eventually draw us into becoming more gracious toward our spouse. Especially in the cauldron of our differences, which can boil with intense frustration at times, it's critical to realize how God views us.

When the differences between mates get painful, we usually see our spouse's flaws or shortcomings as *sin*. But God is not obsessed with our sin, and he doesn't see us as having flaws or shortcomings. He dealt with those completely on the cross. When he sees a lack in our life, he reaches out to us in love, not shame, guilt, condemnation, or anger. He points out the void as the next place he wants to work a miracle.

You see, God has never been—nor will he ever be—disillusioned about you. He never had any illusions about you to begin with. In marriage, we may wrestle with genuine disillusionment in the midst of our battles over whose reality is the right one, but that only means we need to dive deeper into the infinite pool of God's grace.

If we spend our time fighting over our differences, we can lose sight of the grace that God has freely poured into our lives.

Please don't hear me saying, "Anything goes." Marriage involves profound commitment and responsibility. But if we spend our time fighting over our differences, we can lose sight of the grace that God has poured freely into our lives.

For years I saw Diane's differences as a problem or irritation. The longer I walk with her, though, the more I realize she is a perfect balance for my wild and crazy personality. The problem wasn't Diane at all but my limited view of her and of God's work in our lives.

I can only see the beauty of God's design for our marriage if I take the kaleidoscope of our differences and turn it to the light. Standing in a dark corner of the boutique, I couldn't see the view inside the kaleidoscope. Only when I looked toward an open window did it explode with a vibrant display of every color in the rainbow.

How many times in our marriage have I sat in a darkened corner of my own selfishness, wondering what God was thinking when he brought us together? Yet when I turn toward the light of his holiness, love, and grace, he changes everything. Although I may be right about a particular point of an argument, I'm still wrong. My miniscule view of reality seems so pathetic once I allow the light of God's Word to fall on my heart. That's why our sexual relationship has become a reflection of God's gracious work in each of us. As we allow his light to penetrate the deepest, most intimate areas of our lives, we reflect his beauty more and more.

Love Lessons

God's divine design makes men and women unique.

God has created us to be radically different as male and female in certain areas of our lives. We come to see God's magnificent design in bringing us together as we go beyond just accepting those differences. Husbands and wives can only see the beauty of God's purpose for our marriage as we choose to appreciate those differences. When we view them in the light of his creation, our life together becomes a kaleidoscope of his majesty.

God uses marriage as his tool to eliminate selfishness.

Within the context of marriage, our self-centered and selfish attitudes become obvious. We have the choice of remaining as we are and watching our sexual relationship lose its passion and power or following God's plan: death to our selfish desires and new life that renews intimacy and recharges our sex life. Becoming a Sexy Christian involves choice. Wise choices will cause your life—and your sexuality—to more clearly reflect God's character.

Home Play

Rules in review: (1) Avoid "you" statements. Instead, talk about your own actions, thoughts, and feelings. (2) Listen. Don't give advice or attempt to psychoanalyze your spouse. (3) If tempers flare, disengage and pray.

1. The best way to describe our marriage relationship is (circle one):

   a. One of us is Motel 6 and the other is the Ritz-Carlton.
   b. One of us is from earth and the other is from another planet.
   c. One of us is Red Bull and the other is Sominex.
   d. One of us is Ray and the other is Debra (*Everybody Loves Raymond*).

2. My mate and I are a lot alike when it comes to our (circle as many as apply):

   a. hobbies
   b. work ethic
   c. view of finances
   d. sex drives
   e. political views
   f. spiritual ideals
   g. family background

3. The areas of difference that cause the most arguments between my spouse and me are (circle at least two but no more than four):

   a. hobbies
   b. work ethic

   c. view of finances
   d. sex drives
   e. political views
   f. spiritual ideals
   g. family background

4. List two ways you could demonstrate an unselfish attitude in your relationship with your spouse and pray about any changes God wants to bring about. Married couples may choose to share their lists and pray together.

4

Code Talkers

How Can I Speak My Mate's Language?

DIANE

Have you ever visited a foreign country where no matter how hard you tried, communication remained just beyond your grasp? You spoke as loudly as you could, you used all the sign language you could think of, and you still made little or no headway in retrieving the information you needed.

The United States military used this kind of communication barrier to its advantage during World War II when it formed a special group of Navajo soldiers known as Code Talkers. The Code Talkers transmitted messages in a special code based on the unwritten Navajo language. The unique tonal qualities and complex syntax of this language—a challenge for any linguist—made it virtually impossible for the Japanese to decipher American battle messages.[1]

Ted and I faced a reverse version of the Code Talkers early in our marriage when we visited the country of Japan. We had been married only two years when the Navy sent Ted to his first overseas duty station in Iwakuni, Japan. From there he would leave for Vietnam. Just before his Vietnam tour began, I flew to meet him in Japan for two weeks of welcome R and R.

After living apart for nearly six months, we were eager to reach our hotel as soon as we could. That's where we hit the Code Talker barrier head-on. No one—absolutely no one—at the front desk spoke English. We had reserved a room with a double bed, but when we opened the door to our tiny room, we saw two single beds at opposite ends of the room. Of course we couldn't allow this small setback to hamper our time together. We quickly rearranged the furniture and had a honeymoon reunion.

In order to survive those two weeks in Japan, though, we had to become extremely resourceful. The front windows of all the restaurants contained plastic food labeled with the name of each menu item, a convenience we appreciated. When we wanted to order, we grabbed the waiter, walked him outside, and pointed to our selections. God provided other people to help us too. For example, the day we had to take the Bullet Express to Kyoto, we ran into a man who spoke both English and Japanese. He helped us purchase our tickets and sent us on our way.

In Kyoto, the desk clerk could tell the taxi driver where we wanted to go. Getting back to our hotel, however, proved a challenge. Eager problem-solver that I am, I noticed a bowl of matchbooks at the front desk that featured a pen-and-ink picture of our hotel and its name engraved in Japanese. I popped one into my purse, confident I had solved our communication problem.

When it was time to come back to the hotel, we flashed the matchbook and the taxi roared down the road. We were smugly congratulating ourselves on figuring out a way to beat the Code Talkers when we pulled up to a completely differ-ent hotel. The desk clerk explained what happened. We had picked up a matchbook that advertised a sister hotel at the opposite end of town. This Code Talker thing was proving more challenging than we thought.

Rule Out

Seeking clear communication with your spouse can leave you feeling like a stranger in a strange land. Like a Japanese intelligence officer attempting to decipher a Code Talker message, I have sometimes found myself following a pattern that seemed to make sense. *Surely I can beat it, the elusive husband-communication code.* Instead, the code's complexities spiraled into a meaningless jumble, leaving me hopeless, helpless, and a little angry. But like most of marriage, commu-nication works both ways. In his at-tempts to understand me, I'm sure Ted has also longed for the skills of a Code Talker.

Seeking clear communication with your spouse can leave you feeling like a stranger in a strange land.

I've discovered that through the years I often tried to apply the Golden Rule to my relationship with Ted and then wondered why it didn't work. Whether or not we grew up knowing much about Jesus, many of us have heard since our earliest days that "doing unto others as you would have them do unto you" usually gets us where we want to go.

But what happens when we take this as our primary rule for the marriage relationship? If I "do unto" my spouse as I want him to "do unto" me, I'm acting to meet my own needs, not his. As Ted explained in the preceding chapter, male and female brains are wired differently according to the ways God has uniquely designed us. If we follow only the Golden Rule, barriers remain and real intimacy becomes elusive.

Since God created us male and female, he understands our differences and gives men and women specific instructions that recognize those key distinctions. In Ephesians 5:33 Paul challenges women: "The wife must respect her husband." But he gives a different challenge for men in Ephesians 5:25: "Husbands, love your wives, just as Christ loved the church and gave himself up for her." Ted and I believe much of the frustration, dead-end communication, and anger we see in husband-wife relationships comes from ignoring this set of verses. We like to call them the Ephesians Rule.

You understand how the problem occurs. Within every woman's DNA God has placed a heart to love and a desire to belong. No one has to teach us to nurture an abandoned kitten or tearfully empathize with the heroine of the latest romantic chick flick. Men, on the other hand, need admiration and respect. They derive an important part of their self-worth from knowing others see them as capable and competent. In relationships with others, most men find it natural to reciprocate the respect they receive.

I think God displays quite a sense of humor when he makes us one way (to need either love or respect) and challenges us to meet exactly the opposite need in the life of our spouse. The opportunity to meet needs so different from my own challenges me to the depths of my being and uncovers my selfishness every time. And extending my love past the Golden Rule to the Ephesians Rule demands that I learn how to walk in the supernatural rather than in my own strength or natural efforts.

God loves to work in ways that draw us closer to him. If I know I can't accomplish a task, I'm much more likely to call on his strength and to acknowledge his work. God told Paul, "My grace is sufficient for you, for my power is made perfect in weakness" (2 Cor. 12:9). Any couple beyond the first few days of marriage knows how quickly this new relationship showcases each partner's weaknesses. Wouldn't it be wonderful if we could also see it as God intended: a showcase for his strength and victory?

Love Hurts

Let's take another look at Solomon and Shulamith in the Song of Songs. Throughout the first four chapters we witness the unfolding of a great love story. These two are smitten with one another in every sense of the word. Their erotic courtship and marriage flow seamlessly until chapter 5 when Solomon's wife suddenly rejects his romantic overtures with excuses similar to the modern-day "headache" line. She says, "I have taken off my robe— must I put it on again? I have washed my feet—must I soil them again?" (v. 3).

The opportunity to meet needs so different from my own challenges me to the depths of my being and uncovers my selfishness every time.

Do you think Shulamith could have learned something from the Ephesians Rule? We could speculate that maybe she waited up late every night and finally gave up, sad but certain her husband's throne room endeavors took priority over her needs at home. Perhaps she planned a special dinner with candlelight and music, but by the time his camel finally pulled into the driveway the goat roast was dry and tasteless, the harpists long since retired. Shulamith couldn't believe he hadn't at least had the decency to call to let her know of the delay! Before long, his perceived lack of caring and her inferred lack of respect could set them up for a lifetime of responses resulting in more distance and less intimacy.

Patterns like this may be responsible for some recent statistics that say 20 percent of married couples have a sexless marriage. The term *sexless* is clinically defined as having intercourse no more than ten times per year. Another survey of married couples found 33 percent had not had sex in the last month, and 45 percent of couples reported having sex only a few times a month.[2] Sadly, these couples are living more like tired roommates than passionate lovers.

To ensure intimacy in a marriage, both husbands and wives need to see the power of the Ephesians Rule. But how does that play out in our day-to-day living situations? In her book *For Women Only*, Shaunti Feldhahn underlines the power of respect. By interviewing over a thousand men, she found that only one out of four felt actively appreciated and 44 percent of them felt unappreciated at home. The book's most stunning statistic? Ninety-eight percent of men said "getting enough sex" wasn't enough by itself. They wanted their wives to desire them, to long for them sexually. They did not consider a situation in which a wife *agreed* to intercourse merely to accommodate the husband's needs as sexually satisfying.[3]

One man Feldhahn interviewed said about his wife, "She doesn't know how even her occasional dismissals make me feel less desirable. I can't resist her. I wish that I too were irresistible. She says I am. But her ability to say 'no' so easily makes it hard to believe."[4]

I wonder if this also reflects Solomon's feelings as he left Shulamith's chambers after her outburst that night. Over time a wife's seeming lack of appreciation and desire for her husband can actually cause him to spend more hours at work—a place where he feels respected, alive, and on top of his game.

The power of appreciation hit close to home when Ted preached his first sermon over thirty years ago. I was so proud of him, especially since his audience contained many professors from the seminary he attended. They literally leaned forward and hung on every word. Immediately afterward I told him how proud I was and how I sensed the audience responding so positively. I never gave my few words of praise another thought until a week later when Ted told me how much my affirmation meant. I was amazed; he not only re-membered but actually quoted my statements verbatim.

Just as Solomon may have felt the chill from her lack of respect, Shulamith could have felt very insecure concerning her husband's love for her. Scripture tells us she had second thoughts: "I opened for my lover, but my lover had left; he was gone. My heart sank at his departure. I looked for him but did not find him. I called him but he did not answer" (Song of Songs 5:6).

Imagine the regret and insecurity she felt as she looked for her lover, who departed without a word. And how many times does a woman initiate an argument with her husband only to end up feeling rejected when he, sensing her disrespect, turns away or leaves the room rather than tenderly reaching toward her?

A survey from *For Men Only* points out that four out of five women sometimes feel insecure about their husband's love. This insecurity deepens when the husband withdraws or becomes silent. Interestingly enough, a majority of women surveyed said they would be able to give their man space to process a particular situation if he would only take time to assure her of his continuing love.[5]

Language School

In counseling women through the years, I've learned their number one need is affirmation. They need to hear words that say they are loved and appreciated, that their husband finds them attractive (we explore this topic further in chapter 10). Many husbands don't understand the power their words have to take their marital relationship to the next level of intimacy.

In her book *What Women Want Men to Know*, Barbara De Angelis shares a story that encourages men to become Code Talkers in their sexual relationship. She gives an example of a couple she counseled in which the man was very frustrated because of his wife's lack of desire for sex. Individual counseling revealed that the wife often felt used. Since she believed she was only there to meet her husband's sexual needs, her interest consisted primarily in "getting it over with." On a scale of 1–10 (10 being great sex) this wife rated their most recent sexual encounter a 3. The husband, however, rated the same encounter a 9.[6] How could two people see things so differently? Immediately De Angelis recognized the language problem. Hold that thought.

On a vacation trip to Fiji, Ted and I signed up for an all-day kayaking trip. All the kayaks were single-seaters except those paddled by the guides. I volunteered to sit with our guide in the double-seated kayak, certain it would be the safest seat on the river.

Ted often shares that women speak 20,000 words a day and men only 7,000. I had used only a few of my 20,000 that day, and since I had a captive audience, I began asking the guide about his island and culture. As the son of a tribal chief, he was being groomed to become the next chief. He had recently married, so I asked if his wife came from his own tribe. He told me his father had traveled to another island and traded a whale's tooth for his bride, the daughter of another tribal chief.

Right before I asked my next question, Ted pulled alongside us as we glided along the river. I asked the young man if his wife spoke the same language he did. He said, "No, she doesn't, but I am teaching her my language."

At that point Ted began laughing so hard he nearly fell out of his kayak. When he could speak, my husband responded, "I've been trying to teach my wife my language for more than thirty years, and she still doesn't understand." Of course Ted was teasing, but when we first married, that was his attitude exactly. He believed if I could only learn his language and understand the things he considered most important, all would be well. He didn't understand the two-way nature of communication.

Barbara De Angelis (the counselor for the couple who rated their sex life at opposite ends of the scale) recognized that until the husband learned to affirm his wife verbally, their sexual relationship would remain distant. She got the couple back together after a little preemptive coaching with the husband. Then she asked him to explain why he rated that sexual experience a 9. He began to communicate his feelings about his wife by saying how much he appreciated the hard work she put into meeting his and their daughter's needs. He had gone over to hug her because he was so appreciative and became aroused when he noticed her fresh, clean scent and silky hair.

As the husband shared, Barbara noticed the wife's eyes filling with tears. He went on to explain how soft and velvety her skin felt and how sexy and feminine he found her. As they made love, he recalled, he realized again how crazy in love he was.

The wife pulled out a handkerchief and dabbed her eyes. The husband concluded his explanation by sharing his feelings as they finished making love. He couldn't imagine anyone more beautiful than his wife. He felt like the luckiest man in the world, married to this incredible woman whom he loved with all his heart.

The wife, no longer able to contain herself, leaped off the couch and hugged him while crying out, "It was a 10! It was a 10!" This husband, with only a little help, had learned to speak her language.[7]

Solomon, whom the Bible calls a very wise man, speaks his bride's language as he describes his love for her:

> All beautiful you are, my darling; there is no flaw in you. . . . You have stolen my heart, my sister, my bride; you have stolen my heart with one glance of your eyes. . . . How delightful is your love. . . . How much more pleasing is your love than wine, and the fragrance of your perfume than any spice! . . .

Your lips drop wetness as the honeycomb, my bride; milk and honey are under your tongue.

Song of Songs 4:7, 9, 10–11

We can become Code Talkers—adept at a complex language—if we are willing to move beyond the Golden Rule of love to the Ephesians Rule of intimacy. Men can learn to affirm with meaningful words. Women can learn to give their husbands the appreciation and respect they were created to receive. And when we make serving our mate the desire of our hearts, God can supernaturally fill us with his ability to fulfill that desire.

How about it? Are you ready to learn a new language?

Love Lessons

Male-female differences complicate marital communication.

We've already emphasized the divinely designed differences between men and women. The same things that first attracted us to our mates can twist into elements that tear us apart after we marry. Those who seek only to "do unto" their spouse as they would like the spouse to "do unto" them (the Golden Rule) often fail because God created men and women with such different needs. Women's primary need is to be loved, but men require respect.

> *We can become Code Talkers—adept at a complex language—if we are willing to move beyond the Golden Rule of love to the Ephesians Rule of intimacy.*

This explains God's unique prescriptions for husbands and wives in Ephesians 5: "Husbands, love your wives" (v. 25), and "The wife must respect her husband" (v. 33). When we extend the Golden Rule by applying the Ephesians Rule, we meet our spouse's needs much more effectively and open the door for improved communication and intimacy.

God gives husbands and wives the strength we need to communicate effectively with each other.

We cannot properly face the task of marriage in our own strength. We must realize we need the grace of God in order to carry out even the simplest forms of communication. As we surrender our hearts and desires to his control, communication—one of the most challenging aspects of marriage—can become a living expression of Christ's love and care.

Home Play

Rules in review: (1) Avoid "you" statements. Instead, talk about your own actions, thoughts, and feelings. (2) Listen. Don't give advice or attempt to psychoanalyze your spouse. (3) If tempers flare, disengage and pray.

How Hot Is Your Marriage?

Sexual drives often differ, but having a great relationship more than makes up for any gap. Take the analysis below to discover any areas where you may need to heat things up.

1. I do not presume I know what my spouse is trying to communicate.

Always	Most of the time	Sometimes	Never
5	4	2	1

2. When my mate gets angry with me, I am able to listen to his or her side without getting upset.

Always	Most of the time	Sometimes	Never
5	4	2	1

3. We agree about how often we have sexual times together.

Always	Most of the time	Sometimes	Never
5	4	2	1

4. In our relationship there is total consistency between what happens in public and what happens behind closed doors.

Always	Most of the time	Sometimes	Never
5	4	2	1

5. I give my mate my undivided attention when he or she is talking to me.

Always	Most of the time	Sometimes	Never
5	4	2	1

_____ My Score

_____ My Spouse's Score

For Wives to Answer:

6. My husband meets the deepest emotional needs of my heart.

Always	Most of the time	Sometimes	Never
5	4	2	1

7. My husband is very tender to me even at times when I am not respectful of him.

Always	Most of the time	Sometimes	Never
5	4	2	1

8. My husband knows and speaks my love language.

Always	Most of the time	Sometimes	Never
5	4	2	1

9. My husband prays regularly for me.

Always	Most of the time	Sometimes	Never
5	4	2	1

10. My husband has determined to be a lifelong learner of my needs, wants, and dreams.

Always	Most of the time	Sometimes	Never
5	4	2	1

_____ My Husband's Score

For Husbands to Answer:

6. My wife respects and honors me.

Always	Most of the time	Sometimes	Never
5	4	2	1

7. My wife treats me with respect even when I fail to treat her with love.

Always	Most of the time	Sometimes	Never
5	4	2	1

8. My wife knows the things that really make me feel respected.

Always	Most of the time	Sometimes	Never
5	4	2	1

9. My wife honors me in public.

Always	Most of the time	Sometimes	Never
5	4	2	1

10. My wife has determined to be a lifelong learner of my needs, wants, and dreams.

Always	Most of the time	Sometimes	Never
5	4	2	1

_____ My Wife's Score

My Total Score: _____

My Spouse's Score: _____

Final Score (Total of above): _____

Evaluation:

50–45 Skip the discussion and head immediately for the bedroom.

45–40   Try to keep your hands off each other during this evaluation.

40–30   Things are starting to cool.

30–10   You need to relight the fire!

The Power

*Relational and Sexual Power Come
Only through a Truly Intimate
Relationship with God*

5

Hidden Enemy

Why Does My Mate Make Me So Angry?

TED

I sat in my car with the engine running, nervously checking my watch. Just ten minutes remained before I absolutely *had* to leave our driveway in order to make it to the Sunday services. Normally I would have left much earlier, but this morning was different. My wife's car was in the shop, which forced us to travel in the one vehicle we had left.

We had learned long ago that riding together on Sunday morning was a bad idea, but today we had no other options. Diane and I have not only two different brains and perspectives but also two different internal clocks. I always have to be there fifteen minutes early; Diane likes to make a fashionably late arrival. Of course she never considers herself late. In her mind she is always right on time.

Frantically I looked at my watch again. I now had only five minutes before I had to leave or abandon the idea of reaching the pulpit on time. I knew exactly what my wife was up to—she was upstairs making herself beautiful.

The hands of my watch were now moving at a blazing pace. In a mere two minutes I had to go tell everyone about the love of Jesus—assuming I broke every traffic law in the book to get there.

With only one minute left, I couldn't wait any longer. Anger extended its ugly tentacles around my heart as I furiously burst out of the car. I assumed I had placed the transmission in *park*.

I hadn't.

Anxious and angry, I had kept my foot on the brake the entire time. With each passing minute, I had stomped on the brake pedal more forcefully. The car was actually in reverse, so once I stepped out of the car and released my foot, things got exciting. The car lurched backward. As it did, I pushed against the driver's side door to regain my balance, which abruptly launched me back into the driver's seat. That's when things began to move in surrealistic slow motion.

I watched the car door swing wide as I grasped the steering wheel once again. The car began moving down the driveway. Out of the corner of my eye, I caught sight of the basketball pole I had just installed beside the garage. I watched in disbelief as the fully extended door slammed into its steel pole. The car window exploded into a thousand pieces, spraying the driveway with a shower of shattered glass.

Of course I slammed on the brakes, but by now it was too late. The car door bent like a metallic pretzel. I now had a gigantic speed brake extending from the left side of my vehicle. At that exact moment Diane stepped from the house and asked sweetly, "What happened?"

Right before I screamed at the top of my lungs in total frustration, I heard the Lord say, "See what an impatient man you are." Earlier that morning I had experienced a marvelous time with him, praying for the services and the day ahead. At one point I spoke very honestly, "Lord, show me if there is anything you would like to change in my life."

I sat there numbly in a driveway covered with glass fragments and car door parts, a huge lump of anger in my soul. Instantly I realized God had answered my prayer. I mumbled, "Lord, you could have just told me that." He promptly replied, *You weren't really listening, so I decided to give you a graphic illustration.*

Power Surge

A musician had planned to play a song at his own wedding reception. He brought a guitar out and began to tune it while the guests waited quietly. After a few turns of the strings, he told his audience, "It's a little harder to do this with a ring on." A man sitting at a nearby table loudly declared, "*Everything's* harder with a ring on!"[1]

Sexy Christians are folks who are constantly being cleansed and corrected by the Holy Spirit.

That day in the driveway, I found myself learning how hard it is to get to work on time with a ring on. At a deeper level I was realizing that marriage is God's stealth weapon for cleansing the human heart. I felt as though he had taken an industrial-strength scrub brush and started attacking my personal collection of inner grime.

Whether I realized it or not, he was teaching me that Sexy Christians are folks who are constantly being cleansed and corrected by the Holy Spirit. Our sex life becomes profoundly fulfilling when we understand not only the purpose but also the power and passion God intends our sexuality to express.

In this part of the book we will examine the *power* God designed us to experience as a part of biblical intimacy. You see, our loving heavenly Father never intended us to sit in the driveway surrounded by bent metal and shattered glass. He has more for us in our marriages—much more. But far too often we have painful issues in our lives that, like a kink in a hose that keeps the water from flowing, prevent us from experiencing God's power in our relationships. Over the years I've found one of these issues to be so central that if left unchecked it will attack and destroy the power he intends us to have.

Dr. David Schnarch, a clinical psychologist and sex therapist, describes the problem precisely:

> In my professional experience, very often it's hard for couples to achieve sexual ecstasy because they have a mistaken view of what they're looking for. Rather than kinky positions or sexy lingerie, what seems to produce an ecstatic experience is a profound sense of peace. Most of us have no experience of peace while we're having sex.[2]

As we consider this comment, let's take a closer look at the hidden enemy and how it can endanger your sex life. Unfortunately, peace in the sexual relationship is a foreign experience for many Christians. Their lack of understanding about this deadly enemy has paralyzed the growth of intimacy in their marriage.

Heart Attack

Some moments from your past stick with you forever. I remember the following incident from my childhood as clearly as if it happened yesterday.

I had decided to ride my bike over to visit my best friend, Bill, who lived about a mile away. As a kid growing up on a huge ranch in northern California, I didn't have the option of walking down the street to see my friends. A simple afternoon visit required no small effort.

After pedaling across the valley and up their steep driveway, I was huffing and puffing. Bill's mom graciously brought out something cool to drink as we sat on the front porch. Bill's dad joined us. He couldn't stay long, but before he went back out to the fields he paused and looked out over the August beauty of the valley below.

Suddenly he jumped straight into the air and about four feet back from the porch railing. Exploding into the house, he returned immediately with a shovel. He leaned over the rail, looked intently at the flowerbed below, and slammed the tool into the ground. After a few expletives, he reached over and pulled up the still-wriggling body of a four-foot diamondback rattlesnake. Next, he took the shovel back in hand to scoop up the severed head, still attempting a strike with its venomous fangs.

Only moments before, I had walked right past the hidden monster in the flowerbed. Bill's dad didn't mess around. He cut the head off the thing!

Faced with a snake near our front porch, any of us would do exactly as my friend's dad did—taking any measures necessary to eliminate it. Yet so many folks willingly allow things to invade their hearts that have the power to destroy their marriages and sex lives.

In the counseling office I've heard a couple of phrases more times than I can count: "Well, that's just the way I am," or, "That's just the way things are." You know what? I've never heard a story in which someone with a rattlesnake crawling around his house said, "I can't do anything about it. That's just the way things are." No way. Confronted with a poisonous snake, people will do whatever it takes to get rid of the thing, and fast.

So why do we find it easy to dismiss the absolute priority of guarding and cleansing our hearts? This failure slashes deep wounds on the face of our love life and marriage. I want to state this critical truth as emphatically as I can: *Anger is the number one enemy of trust in a relationship, which makes it a total killer of your sex life.*

Scripture also underscores the absolute necessity of guarding your heart. Jesus expresses it succinctly in the Sermon on the Mount: "A good person produces good deeds from a good heart, and an evil person produces evil deeds from an evil heart. Whatever is in your heart determines what you say" (Luke 6:45 NLT). The writer of Proverbs articulates the same truth: "Above all else, guard your heart, for it is the wellspring of life" (Prov. 4:23).

Anger is the number one enemy of trust in a relationship, which makes it a total killer of your sex life.

The Bible makes it clear: we love, live, and work directly from our hearts. In fact, our entire lives flow from that tremendous power source. Unresolved anger—anger within that is ignored or denied—will do more than bend your car door. It will eventually rise up and poison the heart of your marriage. Like the waiting rattlesnake, it strikes suddenly with devastating results. That's especially terrifying because the venom can suddenly flow from your own mouth.

Every husband or wife knows anger comes wrapped right along with the package we call marriage. The Sexy Christian's challenge is not to avoid anger altogether. That's impossible, especially if you love your spouse. But how do you keep anger from becoming the enemy within, lurking in the darkness and ready to release its poisonous venom?

Cut the Head Off the Thing!

The apostle Paul penned some phenomenal insights with respect to anger in our intimate relationships. If you want to understand the real impact of his words, you must also understand the context from which they come.

As he takes pen in hand, Paul sits in a stinking Roman jail cell. No, he hasn't done anything wrong. Instead he is imprisoned for the cause of Christ. Actually, Paul could have easily gotten hot under his clerical collar over the injustice he was experiencing. His writing retreat was not a condo on the beaches of Maui but a maximum security dungeon in downtown Rome. Along the way, others had betrayed and hurt him multiple times. But writing from this dead-end situation, he shows us how to cut the head off the snake and eliminate anger. Regardless of whether you feel any motivation to study Paul's teaching on this topic, I'm sure the people who live with you would celebrate if you finally figured it out.

Read his initial stab at the rattlesnake of anger: "When angry, do not sin; do not ever let your wrath (your exasperation, your fury or indignation) last until the sun goes down" (Eph. 4:26 AMP).

Did you notice? Paul gives us permission to go ahead and be angry. In the original language, this appears as a literal command.[3] Of course some folks have taken this as their life verse. Those people have failed to read the rest of Paul's wise teaching. He tells us there will be times of emotional ups and downs, especially in a marriage. Anger surfaces and stirs up all kinds of things in your head and heart, leading you to make comments to yourself such as: *How could she say that to me? How can he be so insensitive?*

I challenge you in that moment to allow the Holy Spirit to take you beyond your frustration and hurt. Refuse to carry today's anger into tomorrow. In fact, refuse to carry anger any longer than you absolutely must. I say this first because the New Testament teaches it and second because if you refuse to let it go, it can quickly metastasize into a cancer that threatens your entire relationship. We live in such an angry culture that we have trouble grasping how critical this *heart guarding* step is to our marriage. But it isn't an option if you want to have the kind of powerful sex life God has planned for you. And it's certainly not an option if you want to be a Sexy Christian.

After several decades of counseling others, I've realized something: *I have never had to counsel a couple who prays together every night.* In fact, I've conducted a nonscientific survey through the years. I ask every couple right up front, "Do you pray together each night?"

"No. Why?" comes the usual, slightly heated response.

"Oh, nothing. Just checking," I respond. Diane and I have also conducted the same informal survey during our Sexy Christians Seminars. Only about 1 to 2 percent of our attendees indicate they pray together nightly.

After several decades of counseling others, I've realized something: I have never had to counsel a couple who prays together every night.

Now you may say, "But Ted, you probably draw a rather unspiritual crowd." That might be, but a number of pastors and their wives attend these seminars, and only about 2 to 3 percent of them pray together each night. In fact, praying together seems to be a blind spot for most couples.

Why am I making such a big deal out of praying together nightly? For one simple reason: it is nearly impossible to pray with your spouse when you are angry with one another. At those times, Diane and I usually just lie there like two telephone poles, each refusing to touch the other. Eventually one of us realizes how stupid it is for us to stay mad, and we let our guard down in prayer. That brings us both into the presence of God, where anger can never remain. Then we usually have one of those conversations that can last far into the night. Sometimes I think Diane purposely waits until we lie down to bring up the tough things from the day, but I have learned to deal with it. She is following a biblical pattern, and our prayer time together has become a safe place.

Marriage is seldom easy, as the guitar-playing newlywed discovered. But it is more than worth whatever agony comes your way. No joy compares to the transformation from two angry telephone poles sharing a cold bed to a warm couple, lost in the wonder of total trust and love.

Intimacy is the skill of becoming uncomfortably close. It is the challenge of facing our differences, our passions, and our problems at close range. Because we can love so deeply, we can become deeply frustrated with each other. If we fail to process the irritation, we can slide into apathy and indifference, which can become the deepest wound of all.

At one of the first Sexy Christians Seminars we presented, a couple gave us a graphic illustration of this truth. After kicking off the seminar with a great Friday night session, we eagerly pulled into the church parking lot the next morning. Suddenly a silver SUV raced up beside our vehicle. The driver's side window rolled down and the wife declared in strident tones, "That homework assignment you gave us last night as a couple was horrible! We fought like cats and dogs!"

I braced myself for the next barrage of words. Then she smiled from ear to ear and proclaimed, "It was the best sex we've ever had!" Intimacy, real intimacy; the challenge, agony, and delight of it all.

Sometimes, though, you can't resolve the issue no matter how much or how late you talk. This anger is not really about your spouse but about something much deeper. This anger won't respond to a quick fix. In the next chapter we will look at those deeply troubling concerns. Yet Paul's initial statement still rings true. When it comes to our marriage relationship, we must get rid of anger as soon as possible. We must cut the head off the thing!

Love Lessons

Unexpressed anger kills marital trust.

Like a venomous snake lying in wait to attack its victim, unexpressed anger endangers the marital relationship. When it rears its ugly head and strikes, the poison of anger flows. This kills trust and makes true marital intimacy impossible. It also damages and drains the divinely ordained power from the sexual relationship.

Small wonder the enemy loves to sidetrack us by encouraging us to hold on to petty grievances. Without genuine forgiveness, even small or imagined hurts can build up over time, yielding an anger that poisons the heart of the individuals and of the marriage itself.

Prayer makes a great tool to destroy hidden anger.

Paul's words in Ephesians 4:26 give us permission to be angry but admonish us not to use anger as an opportunity for sin. We must guard our hearts against the buildup of anger or it will explode when we (and our spouse) least expect it. The biblical pattern of keeping short accounts by forgiving offenses as soon as they occur helps us guard our hearts wisely.

Most couples, however, neglect the primary heart-healthy measure: praying together as a couple. When you're angry with your spouse, it's tough to pray. That means those who choose to keep this commitment will work together to resolve issues between them. When anger lurks in your marriage relationship, don't mess around. Cut the head off the thing!

Home Play

Rules in review: (1) Avoid "you" statements. Instead, talk about your own actions, thoughts, and feelings. (2) Listen. Don't give advice or attempt to psychoanalyze your spouse. (3) If tempers flare, disengage and pray.

1. The flames of anger can affect every marriage. Which description best fits the way you express anger?

a. controlled burn
b. spontaneous combustion
c. smoldering embers
d. wildfire

In a few sentences, explain why you chose the description you did.

2. The home where we grew up affects our responses years later. Circle the name of the television couple whose conflict management style best represents what you witnessed in your family of origin. Be ready to explain your answer to your spouse.

a. Ricky and Lucy Ricardo (*I Love Lucy*)
b. Tim and Jill Taylor (*Home Improvement*)
c. Dan and Roseanne Conner (*Roseanne*)
d. Howard and Marian Cunningham (*Happy Days*)
e. Cliff and Clair Huxtable (*The Cosby Show*)

3. Fears sometimes lie at the heart of anger. Which of the fears listed below could be possible sources of the anger you experience? (Circle all that apply.)

Abandonment	Loss of control
Rejection	Feeling controlled
Humiliation	Lack of time together
Criticism	Lack of intimacy
Failure	Confrontation
Money or financial issues	Trust issues
Inadequacy	Parenting issues
Lack of communication	Work pressures
Relational issues with extended family	

4. Write a few words to explain a recent example of something (or someone) about which (or whom) you were angry.

6

Catch and Release

What about All the People Who Have Wronged Me?

TED

The snake's glands contained enough venom to kill a thousand men." Gary Richmond's powerful words gripped the attention of the already wide-eyed group of kids at San Diego's Wild Animal Park. As a self-confessed hater of snakes—especially big, poisonous ones—I found myself bathed in sweat as he described a particularly hellacious procedure. A thirteen-foot king cobra was shedding its skin, but a scar kept the clear scale protecting its left eye from falling away naturally. Gary was part of a team assigned to remove the eye cap surgically (a tricky procedure at best). In order to accomplish their task, Gary and four other men had to grab the furious cobra and wrestle with its incredible force.

During a tour in Southeast Asia, I once had the frightening experience of nearly colliding with not one but two of these denizens of disaster. Memories of those encounters rebounded as I tried to wrap my mind around the task Gary so vividly described. And when he quoted the curator's words as the operation neared its close, I knew I would remember them forever. "My hands are sweaty and my fingers are cramping. When I let go, it may not be quick enough. More people are bitten trying to let go of snakes than when they grab them. You get weak quickly when you grab a big poisonous snake."[1]

A Mighty Foothold

Battling the snake of anger can leave us as weak emotionally and spiritually as Gary and his teammates found themselves physically. Paul's words in Ephesians explain why: "For anger gives a mighty foothold to the Devil" (Eph. 4:27 NLT).

Anger toward another person can seem completely innocent at the time we realize its presence. *Come on, he did me wrong*, we rationalize. Over time, however, our anger can grow into an absolute leviathan. This malevolent rage obscures our thoughts so completely that letting go seems impossible.

The devil (literally, "one who accuses") feeds on unresolved anger. When we refuse to process our anger—when we suppress or ignore it—we open a door into our souls. The enemy's accusations now have free access to the innermost part of our being.

The poison stored up from unresolved anger begins its slow release when we blame another person. Before we know it, we are having a hard time sleeping. Every night when we lie down, a steady stream of mental venom pours into our hearts.

Next, we suddenly find new accusations to hurl against the offender. We can't seem to turn our minds off and rest. Over time the warfare damages our soul even more deeply. Subtly, almost imperceptibly, the poison spreads, and we now find ourselves accusing God for allowing the problem to persist.

As the cycle penetrates the core of our being, we even accuse ourselves. In fact, people who carry deep stores of anger become uniquely vulnerable to self-destructive behavior. I have found this especially true in our relationships. We become predisposed to negative thoughts and attitudes toward others. The unresolved anger within becomes a self-fulfilling prophecy. We subconsciously expect others to hurt or be unkind to us, so we live life on guard. In our efforts to self-protect and avoid pain because of our hidden anger, we construct our own emotional prison.

People who carry deep stores of anger become uniquely vulnerable to self-destructive behavior.

The phrases "You owe me," or even "God owes me," sum up the true source of destructive anger. This attitude of entitlement is often the natural response to being wounded by another. We feel as if the individual who wounded us has stolen one of our belongings. Children who grow up in alcoholic families (like the one I came from) end up feeling as though someone made off with a huge chunk of their childhood. I still can't remember significant parts of my grade school and preschool years. The trauma has blocked them from my conscious memory.

If you grew up in a home racked by divorce (as I did), you can feel robbed of the experience of having both parents around. If you grew up in a violent home, you probably feel someone stole your sense of security. If you went through a painful divorce yourself, you may feel your ex-spouse destroyed the promise and potential of finishing this race called life together.

Left to itself, the venom of unresolved anger never disappears. The debt you believe the other person owes you morphs into an open account. You tell yourself through clenched teeth that you'll never close the books until you receive payment in full. And what's the problem? No one can ever pay you in full. You simply carry the anger from one season of life to the next.

For years I did exactly that. Deep within me I carried a burning resentment toward my family of origin. Now don't misunderstand; I loved them incredibly. They are my family. But great love can easily become the breeding grounds for deep-seated resentment.

If you hold on to the snake of anger through the years, it becomes increasingly lethal. Eventually it changes to what I call *free-floating anger*. This type of anger no longer has a conscious source in your mind because you have lost sight of the original cause of pain. Free-floating anger affects even new seasons of your life. For example, you might be getting married or perhaps becoming a parent for the first time, which normally is a time of great joy. But for no apparent reason you find yourself angry with the people closest to you: your spouse, your children, and so on. Although it seems as though these loved ones make you angry, you know deep down that they are not the true source of the problem.

What can you do? The situation seems irresolvable. After all, there's no visible monster attacking your present relationships. Instead, these bonds serve as a trigger point that pulls the rattlesnake up from the hidden flowerbed of your past. The longer you drag that venomous snake of anger around, the more deadly it becomes. The writhing monster even takes on its own camouflage as it buries deeper and deeper within the recesses of your mind.

It took me years, for example, to figure out that the occasional outbursts of anger I directed toward my beloved wife weren't really about her at all. I admit it. I blamed her for the problems every time. But in my heart I knew they had a much deeper source. After about ten years of marriage, I realized my anger was not with Diane but with my family of origin. Diane was safe (she loved me unconditionally) and convenient (she was close at hand), so all the poisonous venom spewed out on her.

This explains why, when I'm taking a couple through the premarital counseling process, I always address the issue of anger. Sometimes the responses amaze me. "Oh sure, he gets angry. Really angry. But I'm starting to get used to it now." Or, "Yes, she throws things and has a fit when she's angry, but I love her with all my heart."

I always smile and say simply, "Get over the *love* thing and run for your life! Run, Forrest, run! God loves your fiancé/fiancée, so you don't have to."

That comment usually gets their attention. Then I point out what you already recognize: people who have this kind of anger directed at them will end up taking blame for things they never did. No matter how much they apologize for what they may or may not have done, the problem won't be settled because it's not about them at all. The true problem is their partner's anger from the past.

A Clean Slate

In Ephesians 4 Paul goes on to tell us that we must get rid of "all bitterness, rage and anger" (v. 31). I checked out the Greek, and guess what the word *all* means? It means *all*. Cut the head off the thing before it kills you!

"But Ted," you might say, "you don't understand my story." I think the apostle Paul would graciously tell you, "Go ahead. Tell me your story; I want to hear it. But after you've shared everything you can remember, I'll still challenge you to let it go."

Sometimes we can feel justified in our anger. We were just kids when someone dumped a truckload of rattlesnakes under the front porch of our lives. Some of us suffered horrendous types of abuse and injustice during childhood. Abuse has no excuse, and we need someone to help us grieve the losses we've experienced. But at the end of the day, you're an adult. *You have to cut the head off the snake of anger, and no one else can do it for you.* If you don't, you'll carry it from one phase of your life to the next. And in the process, its venom will begin to poison your marriage, sex life, and other relationships.

You have to cut the head off the snake of anger, and no one else can do it for you.

"Are you suggesting I just forget about the pain I endured?" you might ask. I have heard that question often as a counselor, and I understand the emotion behind it. In fact, I've asked it many times myself. But if you stop and think about it, nothing anyone can do will ever make up for your pain. I remember asking an angry young man the question, "If your father suddenly turned his life around and came to you and said to you face-to-face, 'I am sorry. What can I do to make up for what I have done to you?' how would you respond?"

"I'm not sure," the young man replied with a puzzled expression. "I've been so angry with him for so long I've never really asked myself what I would do if he changed."

I paused for a moment to let the question sink into his soul before I made the next comment. "The truth is you can't be five or ten or fifteen years old again. Those years are gone. But you can make a decision to clean the slate and start over with your dad."

And that's true for each one of us. It explains why we never seem to balance the accounts in our life. It doesn't matter who we are talking about: a parent, ex-spouse, boss, or friend. There is only one answer to this excruciating human dilemma. Paul uses an exquisite word to describe the solution: "God brought you alive—right along with Christ! Think of it! All sins forgiven, the slate *wiped clean*, that old arrest warrant canceled and nailed to Christ's cross" (Col. 2:13–14 Message, italics added).

The italicized phrase translates one Greek word: *exaleiphein*. It literally means to wipe out.[2] In New Testament times, scribes wrote documents on papyrus. Since the ink they used contained no acid, it did not penetrate the paper. That meant they could sponge off the writing as if wiping a slate. Back then the common way of canceling a debt was to write the letter *chi* on it (today we would say "cross it out"). Instead of asking people to *chi* the sins others committed against them, Paul refers instead to the practice of wiping clean a piece of papyrus. No record of anything written on it would remain.

On the cross, Christ did not simply cancel our debt of sin. He wiped the record against us so clean that there is no evidence it ever existed. God not only forgives but completely eliminates the memory of our debt.

What—beyond the nails—actually held Christ's arms to the cross? Our sins did. Jesus wrapped his arms around our sins and cancelled the debt for sins of the past, present, and future. He allowed his body to be torn to shreds so no record of our sinfulness would remain. His shed blood wiped our record clean.

After nearly thirty years of listening to people's trials and tribulations, you name it and I have heard it. I've listened to some of the most painful stories you can imagine. Unfortunately, horrific tales of abuse, betrayal, and personal pain have become the norm in our hurting world. To be honest with you, at times I get so upset I feel like going out to kill the offending party myself and then getting saved again afterward.

But then I come to my senses. What good would anything like that do? Not a bit—not any more than the other option of keeping an open account on someone who has hurt us deeply. This explains why the New Testament constantly challenges us to forgive "just as God through Christ has forgiven you" (Eph. 4:32 NLT; see also Matt. 6:14; 2 Cor. 2:7; Col. 3:13; 1 John 1:9).

"But you don't know my story!" you may tell me again. You're right; I don't. But you can't have your childhood, your first marriage, or your reputation back. You may have had the rare privilege of actually hearing an apology, but you can never be paid back completely. When you understand and accept this fact, you make a significant step forward in maturity and character. Maturity is not a vague philosophical concept but a trained ability to meet the demands of reality. Therefore, true maturity always includes the ability to forgive deeply.

Power Source

God uses marriage as one of his primary tools for developing maturity in the human heart. The painful, passionate, and perplexing dynamics of marriage bring us face-to-face with the deepest, most hidden dimensions of our hearts. Resolving marital problems, then, requires much more than developing a particular set of skills or techniques. True resolution requires gut-wrenching, soul-shattering personal development. And discovering a deeply fulfilling, incredibly powerful sex life as a couple demands far more than simply learning new touch techniques, improving your communication skills, or rescheduling your time priorities—it requires deep personal growth. A sexual relationship is much more than a one-time event. It encompasses who we have been, who we presently are, and who we can become together.

When a spouse is blind to the ways in which God uses the pains and problems of marriage to mature us, he or she can easily lose hope. If it continues, this hopeless attitude will defeat the marriage. Too often a spouse will give up completely because the pain of the moment seems to have no meaning beyond failure and disappointment, no strengthening of soul and heart. But such a negative perspective comes from the pit of hell—exactly where the enemy wants us to stay.

Having problems in your marriage and your sexual relationship is to be expected. I would go so far as to say it is part of God's plan for you as a couple. Running from the pain and deep pleasure of marriage always results in a profound loss of maturity. Marital pain challenges you—in ways nothing else can—to hear your heavenly Father say to you, "I've got an idea: why don't we close the books on this and forgive them? Let me wrap my arms around you and cover your sins and theirs."

Only forgiveness breaks the power of anger and rage.

Only forgiveness releases the incredible power of intimacy in the marriage of two imperfect people.

Only forgiveness enables marriage to fulfill its ultimate purpose, which is to equip us to live and love in a fallen world.

Only forgiveness enables us to live life with a deep maturity of soul.

You see, God never intended you to smooth over your marriage problems. Often the solutions we seek can only come from living through them and working them out together. That always requires forgiveness. When we avoid the road of forgiveness, we lose. We may escape the immediate situation, but we can't escape ourselves. In the sovereignty of God, our individual crises are custom-tailored, precisely crafted by his hand to confront us with our need for change. When we see our marriage in that light, it becomes an epic drama of godly change and courage instead of a soap opera of anger and bitterness.

Scripture gives multiple amazing examples of how a loving God can structure the crises of our daily struggles as we commit our lives to his care. Sure, we create many of our own problems, but God can start with someone like Joseph—a snot-nosed teenager—and train him to rule a nation. How? He took him from the pit to the prison to prepare him for Pharaoh's palace. That explains Joseph's statement about his brothers' vicious acts: "You intended to harm me, *but God intended it for good* (Gen. 50:20, italics added). Job is another biblical figure who discovered God at work amidst his suffering—not to cause his pain but to use it (Job 42:1–16).

We see this same attitude mirrored in the words of the apostle Paul, who prayed he would come to know the sufferings of Christ so he might walk in the power of his resurrection (Phil. 3:10). And of course Christ is the ultimate example of a life custom-tailored by the Father. His death was decreed before the beginning of time (2 Tim. 1:9), and his sacrifice enables us all to change. Our comfort-oriented culture finds a theology of suffering difficult to grasp, but when we understand our lives are *Father-filtered*, we can find deep peace even in the personal pain of marital conflict.

Harnessing the tremendous sexual power of marriage requires enormous courage as well. If we view sexual desire as merely a biological drive, we assume we should automatically know how to experience intimacy. Many people take this viewpoint despite the fact that humans take longer to reach full sexual maturity than any other species on earth.[3]

A sexual relationship, however, goes far beyond merely experiencing a climax with your mate. I have counseled innumerable couples who were regularly orgasmic but lacked the deep sense of intimacy they craved. Intimacy requires being fully known in the moment. It involves losing yourself in the arms of your spouse and being fully accepted: warts, wrinkles, stretch marks, beer belly, cellulite, and all. All of that demands real courage, which is impossible without a deep understanding of forgiveness.

Hot Topics

When I speak at a men's conference, I can usually read the guys' minds while I am talking about forgiveness: *Come on, what does this have to do with sex?* So I get their attention with this one-liner: "Gentlemen, a woman who understands and can receive forgiveness is really hot!" Then I take them through some research that explores which women are the most sexually satisfied.

Back in 1975 *Redbook* magazine did a study of over 100,000 women and discovered something the researchers couldn't quite understand. In fact, they titled the study "Sexual Pleasure: The Surprising Preferences of 100,000 Women." What surprised them so much was the fact that strongly religious women were *more responsive* sexually than other women. They discovered strongly religious women were less likely than nonreligious women to engage in sexual behavior prior to marriage and more likely to describe their current sex lives as "good" or "very good."[4] In other words, the research showed Christian women can be exceptionally sexy. You might say they're Sexy Christians.

In 1992 a University of Chicago survey of 3,432 Americans between the ages of eighteen and fifty-nine found monogamous married couples registered the highest levels of sexual satisfaction.[5] Who knew?

Later, the National Health and Social Life Survey (NHSLS) came to another interesting conclusion. The researchers found that the public image of sex in America bears virtually no relationship to the truth. In real life, the unheralded, seldom-discussed world of married sex is actually the one that satisfies people the most. The study found that of all sexually active people, married people with only one lifetime partner are the most likely to report they are "extremely satisfied" or "very satisfied" with the amount of physical and emotional pleasure they experience in their sex lives.[6]

Then I tell the men, "When I use the phrase 'Sexy Christians,' I mean it. Those who understand the forgiving power of the cross have a unique advantage in experiencing real intimacy as a couple. And only the grace and forgiveness of God can keep you married for a lifetime."

Forgiveness 101

In chapter 3 we learned that couples who struggle with sexual issues need to learn to trust God and others before they can find true freedom. Such genuine trust can't happen without the power of forgiveness already at work in the relationship. But especially when I'm working with men, I've found I must often unpack the word *trust*, so I've started using the term *emotional integrity* instead.

After all the trauma I experienced early in life, I'd lost touch with my true emotions. On that morning as I stood in the driveway, surrounded by the remains of a mangled car door, it was hard for me to get in touch with my true feelings. Emotional integrity refers to the process of learning to be honest with our feelings again—to connect the dots and reconnect the emotional wires. And it all begins with mature forgiveness, which is also a process. Let's walk through it step-by-step.

1. Identify the source of your anger.

This step is harder than it sounds. We tend to look at our immediate surroundings for a source or cause. That morning in the driveway I was convinced Diane was the source of my anger. But when I really thought about it, I had to ask myself a couple of questions: Did *she* drive the car into the pole? Did *she* leave the car in reverse instead of park?

The obvious answers pointed to the even more obvious source of the problem: *me*. Genuine forgiveness is impossible unless we clearly identify the source of our anger. All too frequently we've lost sight of the original cause, which lies not in the present but in the past.

My need to achieve—a deep-seated desire to succeed—drove my impatience. I believed I had to be at church on time or others would see me as a failure. My concern was not serving God with all my heart, soul, mind, and strength; my concern was (you guessed it) me.

When I finally took the time to examine myself and my anger, I realized all the driveway insanity—and the attitude that produced it—resulted from the accumulated wounds of my past. I had so many father figures and stepfathers who communicated with me in one way or another that I couldn't hack it. No, you're not watching a daytime television talk show, and no, I'm not blaming my parents for my problems. As I honestly sought the source of my anger, I finally began to identify the voices within that had driven me for years and years.

I was responsible for my choices. I caused the car to crash into the pole. But unless I identified the voices within that guided my decisions and attitudes, I didn't have a chance of winning the battle of anger. After all, you can't forgive when you don't know the truth about yourself. Marriage does many things, including providing you with a golden opportunity to discover these deep truths, and fast.

2. Identify your loss (what was taken from you).

Almost everyone misses this step, but it is essential. This process usually takes time, especially if you've been dragging that snake around for a while. You may need to revisit the same issue numerous times. For example, I had wrestled with a father wound in my soul since before I met Christ. I thought after more than twenty years of connecting the emotional wires that I was finished. The Holy Spirit, however, won't give up on us until he brings us into a deep intimacy not only with our mate but also with our heavenly Father.

One afternoon I was putting the finishing touches on a weekend service about the love of Father God. As I triumphantly typed the closing statements on my computer, God spoke to my soul and asked me to give him thanks for my father.

Talk about touching a raw nerve of unexpressed anger! Those words instantly triggered something deep within my soul. You could almost hear the rattlesnake in my reply: "What? Are you kidding? I didn't even know the jerk! He abandoned me at birth!"

The Lord gently repeated his request. *I want you to give me thanks for your father.*

That's when I knew it was the Lord and not a couple of bad pieces of pizza. I stood to my feet, walked into the middle of my office, and simply said, "Dad, thanks . . . for life. I never got to meet you. I would have loved to have known you. I think you would be proud of me. I hope I'll see you on the other end."

Suddenly I collapsed in a pool of tears. This process helped me discover a critical truth: you can't forgive deeply until you've grieved deeply. You have to identify what was lost.

Now, not all grief is good, but good grief is one of the most practical gifts God has given to our fallen world. Bad grief occurs when we repeat the patterns of the past. Let's say I hadn't figured out what I was really feeling when I inadvertently destroyed the car door, so I attacked my wife for causing me to run into the pole. That would result in me experiencing lots of bad grief as I fought through the loss of intimacy with my wife and the pain of hurting her.

Good grief occurs when we recognize the patterns of woundedness or immaturity in our lives and cry out to God for help. I call it *good* grief because it releases healing to those areas of our lives that have caused us so much pain. Good grief is more than good. It's *great* grief because it heals.

Many people fail to connect grief with forgiveness. I remember one counseling session in which I asked a man if he had forgiven his wife. He responded casually, "Sure, no problem."

I pressed further. "Have you really forgiven her?"

He almost shouted his response. "Listen, I forgave her. I'm done with it!"

I replied, "Okay, if you say so, but it doesn't sound like it to me."

As you can tell, he hadn't really forgiven her. The wound was too deep, and he didn't want to face it. He had a religious understanding of forgiveness: an act of the will, something you should do because Christ commands you. *Forgiveness may begin as an act of the will, but in order for it to endure it must reach the heart.* You can't cancel the debt if you never see what was taken from you. And you'll always discover the loss in your heart, not your head.

Forgiveness may begin as an act of the will, but in order for it to endure it must reach the heart.

3. Decide to cancel the debt.

The deeper the wound or debt, the bigger the cancellation ritual should be. When the loss is great, you need to involve your entire being in the healing process. Forgiveness is not a mind game or religious ritual; it must touch the inner recesses of your soul. This may mean you write a letter to the person you need to forgive even if that individual is no longer alive. You may need to list your grievances (what you've lost) on a sheet of paper and burn it as you express your forgiveness. Sometimes the person who needs your forgiveness (such as an angry or abusive parent) is too dangerous for you to confront. In that case, place an empty chair in front of you and talk to the person that way. Express what you've lost but avoid personal attacks.

You see, the simple act of forgiveness matters much more than the specific way you express it. Discover the areas that entangle your soul and learn to seek out these rituals of forgiveness regularly. The God who knows you and your struggles intimately will give you significant and healing ways to process your pain.

Recently I received a call from a man who betrayed me years ago. He asked if I would write an endorsement for a book he is writing. Now I love good books. I love writing and reading them. So I would never treat a book endorsement casually.

I immediately told my friend I would love to write the endorsement. Why? The published book will stand on my office bookshelf as written documentation of my forgiveness. And when the snake wants to crawl back into my heart, I can declare, "The door is closed once and for all. My heart belongs to God and his purposes for my life. You can't touch this."

Love Lessons

Unresolved anger builds up and weakens us spiritually.

Every living, breathing individual carries wounds from the past. Often these wounds have been stuffed deep inside our souls like a snake hiding in a flowerbed. When we don't deal with them, the resultant anger seeps through us like poison and affects every relationship and experience we encounter. The closer we come to another person, the more likely the anger is to spew out and affect them—often unexpectedly and inexplicably.

Even if we identify the true source of our anger, letting go is not as simple as it sounds. By the time we recognize its cause, anger has often wrapped itself so securely around our lives that untangling it requires time, effort, and prayer.

Mature forgiveness is the only true solution to the anger problem.

"Just let it go." How many times have we heard this advice when struggling with a wound or offense? It sounds good, even biblical. But how do we accomplish this task? Mature forgiveness yields emotional integrity—an ability to acknowledge and confront our true feelings.

Like many other aspects of the Christian life, mature forgiveness is a process. It begins with identifying the true source of anger—often a wound from another person or experience. This involves taking a close look at the past for possible causes of unresolved anger. Once the source has been identified, it's time to identify your loss (what was taken from you). Whether you were robbed of a portion of your childhood by alcoholic parents, of your self-esteem by a demanding teacher, or of your identity by the person who sexually molested you, you can begin the process of naming each element and crying out to God for help.

Finally, Sexy Christians who want to express mature forgiveness will face these wrongs or wounds suffered and deliberately decide to cancel the debt—as Scripture instructs, to wipe the slate clean. This often involves a specific ritual such as writing and burning a list of wrongs or meeting with the person who has wounded you to express your forgiveness face-to-face.

My prayer for you as a Sexy Christian is that your life will become one of power and intimacy, not a procession of anger carried from one season to the next. Investing your time and effort in catching the true source of your anger and then releasing it through forgiveness will rev up not only your sex life but every other aspect of your life as well. Go for it!

Home Play

Rules in review: (1) Avoid "you" statements. Instead, talk about your own actions, thoughts, and feelings. (2) Listen.

*Don't give advice or attempt to psychoanalyze your spouse.
(3) If tempers flare, disengage and pray.*

1. Anger often has its source deep in the past. Most of the wounds I received as a child came (circle one):

   a. at home
   b. on the playground
   c. in my classroom
   d. at church

2. Again thinking of your childhood, fill in the blank: When I was growing up, I showed my anger most when _____ did _____ to me. (Change the names if you prefer not to identify a specific person.)

3. Can you think of a time before marriage when someone hurt you but you said or did nothing about it? Write a few words to describe that painful time and prepare to share with your mate.

4. List wounds and offenses for which you need to forgive your spouse, along with one wound or offense for which you feel you need forgiveness from your spouse. When you're both ready, sit together to discuss these points of pain in your relationship. Be careful not to present your comments as an accusation of your mate. Approach the sharing time by saying things like, "I don't understand all that took place, but I felt hurt when ＿＿＿＿＿＿＿＿ happened." Don't use *you* or generalizations like *you always* or *you never* or the discussion can turn into further wounding. And remember, intimacy is a developed skill. If things get heated, disengage. Biblical intimacy is a process, not a single discussion that resolves all our problems.

7

Getting Up Off the Floor

How Does My Inner Pain Affect Intimacy?

TED

Ted, you are one sick puppy, I told myself. That was the moment I cried out to God for help. And at that exact moment, the old yellow linoleum floor suddenly came back into view.

It was clearly a gift from the Holy Spirit because I hadn't thought about the floor of my adolescent bedroom in years. Each tile was stamped with a shoddy Florentine pattern, its tiny grooves filled with old wax. I watched as a brilliant drop of blood splattered onto one grimy square.

The blood was mine. I had walked into my parents' bathroom only a few minutes before. Apparently my stepfather had grown tired of beating my mother. After dragging her into the bathroom, he began pouring water over her face in a horrific attempt to drown her.

I'd had enough, and—at 120 pounds dripping wet—I stepped in to defend Mom. My stepdad's bulk more than doubled mine. He spun around, slamming his fist into my face. The impact sent me flying down the hallway. I got to my feet and he was on me in an instant. This time he knocked me into my room. I started to rise once more. He leaned over me, snarling, "If you get up, I'm gonna kill you!"

Survival Mode

I was no fool. I wasn't about to get up. But right there, as I watched my blood hit the linoleum, I made a vow: *I will never let another man treat me that way as long as I live.* On that day, any final remnants of gentleness plunged to the depths of my heart. From that moment on, I became a survivor.

Survivors have to look the best, do the best, be the best— or make others believe those lies are true. For the survivor, high school and college sports are never about the joy of the sport; they are always about beating other men. My years in the Marine Corps followed this exact pattern. I fought hard to gain the acceptance of one company of men while learning to defeat others. Anything I did, including serving my country, always carried my hidden personal agenda.

Especially when it comes to relationships, the survivor mentality is incompatible with vulnerability. In fact, survivors can never find true intimacy with another person because they are always on alert. They're waiting for that next punch to fly, that next drop of blood to hit the linoleum.

Have you ever met someone who enjoys—maybe a little too much—a reputation as a deeply spiritual person? This person may go so far as to claim prophetic insight and knowledge but somehow never seems able to get along with fellow believers. People like this make communication challenging and intimacy impossible. They lack the maturity of a genuine walk with Christ. The truth is that they are not prophetic but puerile. They hide their spiritual immaturity behind a mask of religious language. They can't take time to grow up enough to seek true intimacy because they are always on the alert. They are survivors.

In the same way, if someone claims to have an intimate walk with Christ yet participates in sexual sin (such as having sex outside of marriage, viewing pornography, or having an emotionally adulterous relationship in a chat room), this person is not only spiritually immature but also a survivor who uses sexual sin to medicate inner pain. To underline the destructive nature of this choice, Scripture describes this person as "deceived" (Titus 3:3). The public display of a walk with Christ is actually a carefully orchestrated mask designed to conceal a life of deception. Something has happened to this person in the past—like my close encounter with my bedroom floor—that defines the future. From that moment on, a person like this lives as a survivor: immature, invulnerable, and seemingly incapable of intimacy with anyone.

Early in my pastoral career, I found myself serving God yet still controlled by the impact of a stepfather's fist more than thirty years earlier. I'm sure that's why God brought the picture back up in my memory. The reality check began with some words from Diane—words I had heard many times before. "You're too driven," she kept telling me. "You never seem to be able to relax and enjoy life. You're always competing, even when there's no one to compete against."

As usual, my wife was right. At first, though, I dismissed her observations. Of course I was competitive! She just didn't know what I knew. For example, how could she possibly understand the intense pressures of my job?

Her words kept ringing in my soul because even though I avoided true intimacy, I could never ignore her love for me. Several months later as I sat in a seminar for pastors, her caring words finally hit home. I realized I had walked into the room and unconsciously evaluated all the other leaders according to the size of the churches they served. Without even thinking about it, I placed myself in competition with every man in that room, just as Diane had tried to tell me so many times.

When I recognized this terrible truth, I cried out to God for help. That's when, more than thirty years later, I saw the blood hit the floor once again.

Peeling the Onion

During my days as a military pilot, I always preferred the quick fix. I wanted to get back in the sky and get on with the battle. That's probably why I thought this new insight from the Holy Spirit would suddenly make everything better. From then on Diane and I would automatically walk lovingly together into new levels of intimacy and sexual fulfillment. Right?

Real intimacy involves a journey—our journey with God and with each other—much more than a destination.

Wrong. Real intimacy involves a journey—our journey with God and with each other—much more than a destination. Through the years I have discovered that dealing with deep wounds (and we all have them) is never a quick fix. Instead it's much more like peeling an onion. With every layer you confront the pain and shed a few tears. Every time you think you might finally be finished, you find yourself peeling back another layer of hurt. This doesn't mean you are a basket case; it means God is healing you much so you can love much (Luke 7:47).

Science verifies the impact of these multiple layers of hurt. The Canadian Institute of Neuroscience discovered that when an adult has experienced pain and trauma at some point in the past before the brain was fully developed (generally before twenty-five years of age),[1] strange things can happen, including the mental intrusion of the past into the person's present. The study summed up the results of early childhood trauma by saying, "Past trauma can disturb the mental and behavioral functions of adults by mechanisms that they cannot access consciously."[2] In other words, we carry the wounds of our childhood into our adult life. Because these memories are so deeply imbedded, they can influence our reasoning processes at the unconscious level. For example, when I became violently competitive as a young adult, I made no conscious connection to that behavior and the abuse I suffered at the hands of my stepfather. Of course he did not cause my poor choices; I made those decisions myself. But when we don't understand or recognize the software downloaded into our heads in childhood, we end up fighting battles we can't win. The Holy Spirit can help us understand what drives us even at an unconscious level.

In the late nineties, Kaiser Permanente Hospitals and the Centers for Disease Control (CDC) carried out an illuminating research project. It was the largest study ever done on the way family background affects adult health. The researchers identified ten adverse childhood experiences (ACEs) that could impact a child's life. In order to determine what effect these ACEs have on a person's physical health, they examined the health records of seventeen thousand individuals and compared them to the number of ACEs they experienced.

The results were striking. The team discovered that the higher the number of ACEs a person had experienced, the greater the loss of health in adulthood and the higher the number of addictions. They concluded that heartache and hurt within the home often prepares the soil of addiction and illness.[3]

That explains why prior to meeting Christ I was rapidly headed right off the cliff into alcoholism and sex addiction. And it explains why God turned my thoughts back to the linoleum floor.

Impulse Control

It doesn't matter how mild or severe the blow may have been. When we don't deal with the trauma we've experienced, we have trouble getting up off the floor. In addition, we have a tendency to become very impulsive in our approach to life.

What difference does impulse control make? In one of the most intriguing developmental studies ever conducted, Walter Mischel of Stanford University created a simple test of the ability of four-year-old children to control their impulses and delay gratification. Researchers took a group of children, one at a time, into a room with a one-way mirror. Next, one marshmallow was placed on a table in front of the child. The child was then told that the researcher had to leave and that the child could have the marshmallow immediately, but if he or she waited for the researcher to return, the child could have two marshmallows. After the researcher left, some children grabbed the marshmallow within seconds. Others waited as long as twenty minutes for the researcher to return.

In a follow-up study, the children were tested at age eighteen. At that time comparisons were made between the half of the children who grabbed the marshmallow ("impulsive") and the half who delayed gratification in order to receive the enhanced reward ("impulse controlled"). The half of the children who were most impulsive at four years of age scored an average of 524 Verbal and 528 Math on their SATs. In comparison, the controlled students scored 610 Verbal and 652 Math.

A single observation of four-year-olds accurately predicted this astonishing 210 average point difference in scores. Even at four years of age, a child's decision to gobble a marshmallow now or wait to receive two marshmallows later turned out to be a better predictor of future SAT scores than IQ. The researchers also found that the self-controlled group turned out to be more socially competent, with a higher level of self-esteem and a lower level of divorce later in life.[4]

No Small Marshmallows

Why have I cited all this scientific data? Only to stress that the profound biblical truths that define our relationships are clinically verifiable issues. The trauma and abuse you experienced in your family of origin can set you up for health problems and addictive, impulsive behavior as an adult. Although the marshmallow experiment didn't investigate whether the children who behaved impulsively were reflecting the structure of their homes, it certainly seems likely. The bottom line: *impulsivity can have a crippling effect on your life.*

Impulsive people end up with lives of mediocrity instead of excellence and with marriages that are tolerably Christian rather than deeply intimate. If you want to move into health, you must face your impulsivity. And that means you must face the pain within. Peeling the onion can hurt; the layers can be painfully difficult to separate. The acrid odor slices the air, and the process invariably makes you cry. But that day in the pastor's conference, staring down at the blood-spattered linoleum again, I finally got it. I suddenly realized that if I didn't get up off the floor and address these wounds from the past, my marriage would never experience real intimacy. I would pass on a habit pattern that would cripple my kids as well.

And what about impulse control? Simply put, the temptations Satan lays before you are not small marshmallows. Your ability to delay gratification has huge implications in every facet of life. This includes the power of your sexual relationship and the intimacy you may or may not experience.

Impulsive people end up with lives of mediocrity instead of excellence and with marriages that are tolerably Christian rather than deeply intimate.

Trying extra hard to avoid the marshmallows of life simply doesn't work. The only way you can withstand the world's array of junk food temptations is to make sure you consistently fill yourself with the good stuff. No, you don't need a special way to reach God, and you don't need to rack up some sort of spiritual brownie points. Instead, you must develop the ability to enjoy your Papa God regularly. You need to embrace this critical life skill because, sooner or later, we all have to deal with pain.

Marriage, as part of God's design to build his character within us, can be extremely painful at times. If you aren't regularly enjoying God, you will be profoundly vulnerable to the temptation to medicate your pain by acting impulsively. You may bypass the filter and look at a porn site or waste your entire lunch hour scanning the magazines in an adult bookstore. You may respond with sudden fury to a small mistake by your spouse or your child. You may decide to self-medicate with a quick shopping trip—to the tune of hundreds of dollars on an already-overflowing credit account. In any of these downward-spiraling scenarios, intimacy rapidly becomes impossible. Trust is destroyed, and the beauty and power of the sexual relationship is lost.

I recognized my bottom line when God brought the blood on the linoleum floor back into focus. He revealed it so simply that even I could understand it: I had to get up off the floor! I faced a huge challenge in dealing with something to which I did not necessarily have conscious access. But I realized that if I was ever going to enjoy God completely, if I was ever going to experience the intimacy Christ promised for our marriage, I needed help beyond myself. I was fighting a battle in which I couldn't even consciously see my foe. In that situation, how do you win?

Fight to the Finish

Fortunately, the apostle Paul gives us some wise counsel. First, he graphically describes the battle of the mind that we all face—the battle against the forces of hell and hurt in our fallen world: "This is no afternoon athletic contest that we'll walk away from and forget about in a couple of hours. This is for keeps, a life-or-death fight to the finish against the Devil and all his angels" (Eph. 6:12 Message).

Paul understood the heat of the battle. He also understood the source of the victory. We see this in the advice he gives, appropriately couched in military terms: "Put on salvation as your helmet, and take the sword of the Spirit, which is the word of God. Pray at all times and on every occasion in the power of the Holy Spirit" (Eph. 6:17–18 NLT).

First, Paul tells us to protect our thought processes by consciously choosing to remember that Christ shed his blood for us. Our Lord's love for us is so outrageous that he allowed himself to be brutalized for our sin. My blood spilled on the linoleum that day in my youth was more than covered by Christ's blood shed on the cross for me. Sure, I experienced injustice, but Christ experienced the ultimate injustice for me. Recalling his sacrifice and the great love that motivated it would garrison my mind against the enemy's attacks.

Paul does not present us with a passive picture, telling us to forget our past struggles and move on. Instead he challenges us to take up the "sword of the Spirit, which is the word of God." The phrase *the word of God* doesn't just point to a passage of Scripture. Here Paul uses a very distinct Greek word—*rhema*—which refers to a word that God the Father speaks personally to us out of his eternal Word.[5]

As we begin learning to understand and apply this word of the Lord, it has the potential to bring healing to the core of our being. Through the power of his Holy Spirit, it reaches down into the subconscious processes of our mind, bringing life to our soul. Again, I am not referring to a spiritual quick fix in which a deep-seated problem is solved in a moment. We're dealing with wounds that may go all the way back to our childhood. As the Kaiser Permanente/CDC research showed, incidents that lie deeply burned in the recesses of our brains can profoundly affect our physical health and ability to relate in the present. Although we may not have immediate conscious access to these memories, they have a far-reaching impact upon our life today.

Only one weapon is powerful enough to confront and heal these deep wounds of the past. No wonder Paul refers to the *rhema* of God as the sword of the Spirit. Whenever Diane and I work with people who are battling these wounds, we encourage them to develop a rich habit of feeding on God's Word. We teach them how to journal from Scripture, taking a small portion each day from God's love letters and entering into a dialogue with their heavenly Father. This is not difficult and can take as little as thirty minutes per day.

As you take up the sword of the Spirit, he uses it as his instrument of power in your life. This power can lift you up off the floor when life has knocked you down. In reality, your Father not only wants to give you a *rhema*—he wants to become your *rhema*, working his Word deep into your heart, mind, and soul.

> *Your Father not only wants to give you a rhema—he wants to become your rhema, working his Word deep into your heart, mind, and soul.*

But how do you complete the process? What enables you not only to get up off the floor but also to stand in victory as the enemy continues his assault? To find the answer, let's return to Paul's words in Ephesians. The third section of his battle plan reads, "Pray at all times and on every occasion in the power of the Holy Spirit" (Eph. 6:18 NLT).

When I returned to the United States from Vietnam, I thought everything in my life would return to normal. I could never have been more wrong. Almost immediately I faced tremendous attacks on my spirit in the form of intense flashbacks. Sometimes I woke up covered in sweat from reliving the horrors I had seen in combat. Interestingly enough, occasional memories of the confrontation with my stepfather intermingled with the terrifying images of my experiences in the heat of the battle. As I began spending time in the Word, God brought me a renewed sense of his care. I began to understand that his great love for me was moving him to bring health and healing into my life.

As I asked my Papa God to help me deal with this pain, I sensed him challenging me to begin praying in the power of the Spirit—particularly each night as I fell asleep. It was as though he was telling me that he would fight the battle for me while I slept. He alone could reach down into the unconscious depths of my soul and bring healing. The power of his Spirit was doing what I could not do on my own. Within a couple of months the flashbacks stopped, and I've never had another one. That began a continuing effort in my life to practice the presence of Christ through prayer.

Yes, it's a fight to the finish, but it's also a healing process. The steps Paul prescribes are part of a continuing battle plan, not a checklist to complete as quickly as possible. God wants to work healing into your life as part of his ongoing relationship with you. The secret to getting up off the floor and to new power in your sexual relationship is true intimacy with God and with your spouse. This Ephesians 6 process is a way to move toward that intimacy. Your ongoing walk with the Lord will lift your marriage to new levels of closeness day after day.

Open Up

I've led hurting folks through this exact sequence over and over again. It doesn't matter if it is a wife who can't respond sexually to her husband because of abuse in her past or a big burly guy who pours concrete for a living. Neither one can face the challenge of opening up to another person.

You recognize the problem, don't you? The wounded wife and the tough-as-nails husband have the same problem. A child is hiding within each of them—a child who was knocked to the floor years ago. That child finds it impossible to get up off the floor long enough to open up to a marriage partner and experience deep intimacy with the spouse God has provided. But we have hope in the one who is our hope. No one has to stay on the floor. Developing and honing the skills for the battle will totally change your love life with God as well as with your spouse.

Let's reexamine our understanding of biblical intimacy. First, this kind of intimacy involves self-confrontation. Out of this comes self-disclosure to your partner, which results in a unique closeness. And this explains why marriage is such a magnificent personal growth tool in the hand of God. Ultimately it is an experience of tripping over your own weaknesses as you reach out for true oneness with your spouse. Only then can you find its real power.

To see marriage in any other light is to live in a fantasy world. And all too soon the jagged shards of reality will shatter such a world. Often we encounter these shards when our marriage partner makes observations about us—as Diane did when she told me I was too driven.

Other than God himself, no one has a better perspective on our true identity than our spouse. The problem comes when we readily dismiss our spouse's observations about us because we know their own weaknesses so well. This quickly becomes a vicious cycle of reacting to one another, which leads to a relational stalemate. You've heard the old joke: "How can you tell the longest-married couple at the restaurant? They're the ones not talking to each other."

Couples who aren't yet married can't seem to *stop* talking to each other. Most people would say the silent marriage partners have a communication problem. That's not usually the case. Most often they are already communicating clearly. They just don't like the messages they hear. They know what their spouse is going to say and they stopped listening long ago.

As you get up off the floor, ask God to give you the grace to open up to him as you seek him through his Word and prayer and then to open up to your spouse. God often uses your mate to help you realize something is terribly wrong. He did not create you to lie on the floor, bruised and broken by the wounds of your past. He came to give you life, and life abundantly (John 10:10). When you take this truth and apply it to your marriage, the possibilities are incredible.

Beginning of the End

I recall another important event in my journey of healing. I had recently decided to follow Christ and suddenly found myself caught in the middle of a rocket attack on the ground. That terrifying moment galvanized my realization that *I am not the master of my fate, the captain of my soul*. Later, following my tour of duty in Vietnam, I was assigned to a squadron in Japan for a couple of months before they sent me home. It was routine flying, just staying proficient on the aircraft, but God was about to start the healing process.

It was the middle of winter in Japan, where the weather can change in a moment. I could see a huge front approaching the airbase where I was scheduled to land. As a precaution, before I began the descent I checked with the controller to see if the weather had closed in on the airfield. He said that the front hadn't reached the base and it didn't look as though it ever would, so I dumped fuel and headed down. That decision sealed my commitment to land. The front chose that moment to make its appearance. After three attempts, with each pass going ever lower in search of the newly obscured runway, I decided it was time to head for my alternate field.

When I requested directions, the tower informed me that the bad weather had closed in that field too. With fuel for only a few more approaches at best, my options suddenly went from grim to grotesque. I could eject and freeze to death in the Sea of Japan (in this kind of weather it would take a search team forever to find me) or, equally daunting, keep flying downward until I either found the runway or struck the ground.

I decided I preferred a sudden but warm death, so I started one more approach. I had made up my mind: this was the final shot, one way or the other. I slipped downward to four hundred feet . . . three hundred feet . . . two hundred . . . one hundred . . . seventy-five feet! At the last instant I saw the runway coming up, dropped the tail hook, and slammed into the arresting gear at the approach end of the runway.

I retracted the tail hook and taxied off the still-invisible runway purely out of habit. As I paused for a moment, my legs began shaking so violently that I could hardly steer the plane. It suddenly hit me: I was alive for a reason. In all my years of combat, I had never once thought about it, but this storm out of nowhere got my attention.

Wake Up!

Does God have your attention yet? Sometimes, before we can get up or begin to open up, he has to wake us up and show us that potential brush with death. In my case, realizing that I had escaped death for a reason set me on the journey of seeking him in fresh ways. It moved my focus from the physical battle to the much greater one taking place in the spiritual realm. And as I returned to the States and began to follow God's battle plan from Ephesians 6, I began to see his healing take place in my own life.

But what does this have to do with sex? (Guys, I hear you.) The answer is—everything! As husband and wife, not only are we responsible to God for our own healing, but we also must have the integrity to help each other wake up and begin to deal with our own "linoleum moments" as well.

Admiral James Stockdale, one of my heroes, was imprisoned in the Hanoi Hilton for seven years. He was flying the same aircraft I did when he was shot down over North Vietnam. As the highest-ranking officer in that dreaded prison camp, he was tortured numerous times. Yet he never gave in to his tormentors and consistently led the resistance against them.

When asked how he was able to withstand such a long struggle for freedom, he made this incredible observation: "You must never confuse faith that you will prevail in the end—which you can never afford to lose—with the discipline to confront the most brutal facts of your current reality, whatever they might be."[6]

This thing called biblical intimacy will be one of the greatest challenges you have ever faced. Today's culture is awash in sexual temptations, and instant gratification has become a way of life for many. Once you have come to Christ, the journey back to sexual health can be a torturous challenge. (For more specific information, see appendix 1, "Sexy Christians: Woman to Woman," and appendix 2, "Sexy Christians: Man to Man.")

Exiting a lifestyle focused on immediate sexual gratification will test you to the core of your being. But you must wake up and face your current reality, no matter how brutal it seems. You must discipline yourself to respond to the Holy Spirit's leading as he deals with those things that have kept you from getting up off the floor and opening up to your spouse. Never lose faith in the fact that he will not only lead you but will be right there with you on every step of that journey, no matter how severe the bondage or how brutal the wounds from the past.

I can assure you that the result is worth every moment of the battle. *As you and your mate grow in genuine biblical intimacy, you'll discover an incredible sexual power*—the synergy that comes from truly knowing one another. Remember Shulamith, the captivating bride mentioned in chapter 1?

In the third chapter of the Song of Songs, she warns other women not to awaken love until the time is exactly right (v. 5). The next six chapters in this book are a beautiful—and beautifully open—portrait of that awakening.

Sexy Christians, it's time to wake up, get up, open up—and let the celebration begin!

Love Lessons

Childhood wounds hurt, but warfare tactics help.

Childhood wounds can have long-term effects, as shown by more than one research study. In terms of sexuality, what does this mean? Specifically, it means that we need to wake up to our need for God's intervention, get up off the floor where we remain trapped by old wounds, and open up to our spouse in true biblical intimacy. We do this through the means of spiritual warfare: identifying with Christ's shed blood, applying the specific word of God (*rhema*) to our lives, and praying at all times in the power of the Spirit. As God takes us through this process, he pours new sexual and spiritual power through our relationship. That gives us a reason to celebrate!

Home Play

Rules in review: (1) Avoid "you" statements. Instead, talk about your own actions, thoughts, and feelings. (2) Listen. Don't give advice or attempt to psychoanalyze your spouse. (3) If tempers flare, disengage and pray.

1. Following the story that opens this chapter, Ted describes himself as having a survivor mentality because of the wounds received in his youth. Reread his description of survivors (page 108). Do you know someone who thinks or acts this way? Without naming the individual,

describe the actions that cause you to see this person as a survivor.

2. Ted compares the process of healing to peeling an onion. Color the layers of the onion pictured below from the outside in to show how far you believe God's healing grace has penetrated into your life.

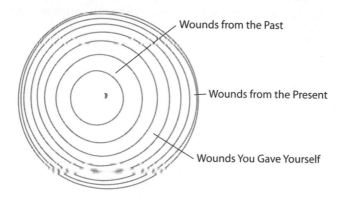

3. Ted realized many of the family patterns of the past were affecting him in the present. Use this exercise to help identify some of the family patterns you grew up with and which ones you see yourself repeating in the present.

> Circle "F" if you saw these behaviors in your family of origin.
> Circle "P" if you see these behaviors appear in your present relationships.

F P Controlling behavior
F P Criticism or judgment of others
F P Blame or defensiveness toward others
F P Black-and-white thinking

F P Codependent behaviors (needing others to make you happy)

F P Attempts to receive love or to feel valued through pleasing others

F P Addictive behaviors: food, sex, work, overactivity, shopping, alcohol, drugs, gambling

Take time to discuss with your spouse how any of the behaviors you circled may affect your relationship as husband and wife.

8

Clipped Wings

Why Won't My Relationship Work?

TED

Some aircraft accidents defy description. I saw several of those as a student pilot. At that time the Navy was rushing us through training and out the door because a war was on. In fact, we sometimes trained on planes that had actually flown in the combat fleet but for one reason or another had been retired. Sometimes these veteran planes caused problems—like the one encountered by another student pilot as he completed his final phase of training.

Suddenly this young pilot found himself in a severe, nose-to-the-ground altitude plunge. In a panic, he snapped back on the controls, pulling hard to bring his craft back to a normal flight pattern.

What the student didn't know nearly killed him. The plane had developed corrosion deep inside its wing structure due to the saltwater environment of the carrier that had housed it for so long. When the pilot yanked back the controls, he put a huge stress on the corroded section and a portion of the left wing promptly snapped off. The loss of pressure threw him violently around in the cockpit as the plane rolled to the left. Next, the severed piece flew off against the right wing, breaking off a section of it as well.

The pilot and his damaged plane dropped out of the sky like a rock. He kept applying more power until, at full throttle, he was literally standing the plane on its tailpipe. Since he couldn't see the wings, he had no idea what had happened. He only knew he had limited control and had to apply maximum power in order to remain airborne. But soon, maximum power would mean minimum or no fuel. He used the radio to scream for help.

Quickly, authorities instructed the student to head back to home base and perform a flyby so they could diagnose the problem. I wasn't there to see it myself, but others told me that until his craft appeared on the horizon they assumed they had another overanxious student pilot, panicking and exaggerating his problem. Imagine the stunned silence as he flew by at full throttle, only a stub of each wing protruding from the sides of the aircraft. Soberly, the ground team instructed him to fly to an uninhabited area and eject as soon as he could.

We don't have the option to eject when we face problems in our personal lives. Hold on to that thought—and that story—because we'll talk about it again soon.

Falling Apart

After reading through the previous chapters, you may wonder how Diane and I are doing in our marriage relationship. Granted, we had quite a rocky start, but eventually we came to understand one another perfectly. We've now taught numerous classes and seminars on intimacy, so we've worked through all of our disagreements. Finally, we serve in the ministry together. Of course we're so spiritual we never have any conflicts.

Not!

As you probably realize, Diane and I have battles just as you do. Why does that happen? I've asked myself that question at least a million times in over forty years of marriage. Fortunately God's love letter, the Bible, provides a very clear answer.

The battles go all the way back to the beginning—back to the Garden of Eden. When Adam and Eve decided to do their own thing, they set in motion a relational whirlwind that affects us still. In fact, you can tell exactly when couples get caught in the Adam-Eve spin. It occurs the moment they choose not to trust God.

Let's go back to the Garden. When God asked Adam what had happened, he gave the first of a long succession of lamebrained husband excuses: "The woman you put here with me—she gave me some fruit from the tree, and I ate it" (Gen. 3:12).

Does Adam's response remind you of anyone you know? When God asked what he had done, he immediately changed the subject and blamed the woman. When Diane lets me get away with it, I like to tell people that the woman blamed the snake and the snake didn't have a leg to stand on.

Theologians call Genesis 3 "the fall." This horrific event lies at the heart of the verbal wars that so easily erupt between husbands and wives, parents and children, coworkers, and even total strangers. When you think of the fall of humankind, think back to that stub-winged aircraft suddenly dropping out of the sky. It didn't have a chance to fly normally because, unbeknownst to the student pilot at the controls, hidden corrosion had caused irreversible damage and, in effect, clipped its wings. The plane was literally an accident waiting to happen.

This story graphically portrays our spiritual condition. Imagine this: Diane comes into my study at home and interrupts me while I'm preparing a lesson entitled "The Love of God." I turn and say something rude or curt so I can get back to my important work. As she turns and walks out, I say to myself, *Now, why did you do that?* I love this woman so deeply, yet I can make some truly ridiculous statements. At times I've even blamed her for a disagreement *I* chose to begin. What happened to our wings of intimacy?

I is the fundamental mantra of all people in this hurting world who try to fly under their own power.

Through the years I've thought hard about this struggle. Over and over again I have found myself at full throttle in my commitment not to do or say anything unkind to my wife when, before I realized it, I blew it. Every time I ended up falling like a rock because of my own ridiculous comments.

I began to notice, however, that in the process I was whispering certain things to myself prior to opening my mouth. My self-talk indicated some deeper issues; I had corrosion within. I told myself things like:

> *I need to get something done. . . . I can't talk now.*
> *I want to go to this place, not that one.*
> *I don't want to go shopping. I really don't want to go shopping!*
> *No, I don't want to watch a "chick flick."*
> *I want to use the money this way, not that way.*

Do you notice a predominant pronoun in those statements? That's right: *I. I* is a favorite pronoun of fallen folks—people with clipped wings. And *I* is the fundamental mantra of all people in this hurting world who try to fly under their own power.

Let's take it one layer deeper. Did you catch the dominant attitude in my inner dialogues? Again, it's a common perspective shared by every clipped-wing person: *I'm right and you're wrong!*

We've moved from noting the differences between the male and female mind to examine some very challenging issues. The issue of wounds and family patterns of the past can be tough, but nothing is as difficult to face as our own fallen condition. According to the apostle Paul, we all struggle with that whether we recognize it or not: "For all have sinned; all fall short of God's glorious standard" (Rom. 3:23 NLT).

In our journey toward intimacy, we instinctively try to get our spouse to listen to and accept or validate us. Instead, we need to listen to ourselves. If we hope to soar on the wings of full, powerful intimacy, we have to realize the extent of the battle. The figure below depicts the issues you must address on your journey toward true intimacy.

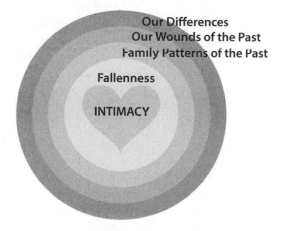

It's All about—Me?

Can you tell that a large part of my counseling ministry involves moving people out of their comfort zones? You

should see the shocked reactions I get when I tell someone who has come to me for help, "Forget about working on your relationship." That's because most people think the relationship is the ultimate problem. Their idea of "working on the relationship" is code for "improving my partner." But that self-centered approach only leaves them more frustrated and farther from the intimacy they seek.

When you work on yourself, you're working on your marriage. If you change, your relationship will eventually change.

Frustrated partners don't get what they want from the marriage relationship because, fundamentally, they're not getting what they want from themselves. *When you work on yourself, you're working on your marriage.* If you change, your relationship will eventually change. Sure, there are some exceptions—such as a partner who is locked into abusive behavior. But the key to resolving most marriage problems does not include changing the other person first. Guess where change must begin?

A discerning element deep within the soul of every lover of God instantly recognizes truth when someone confronts us with it. As a pastor and counselor, I do my best to speak directly to that discernment. When my counselees listen to and act on my challenge to confront truth in their own life, they usually find that their spouse becomes less adversarial. Still, it can be difficult to refocus on changing ourselves rather than our spouses.

The following email sent to Diane shows what can happen when one spouse attempts to change the other. It speaks for many women who struggle with corrosive issues that threaten to drive them and their husband apart. Some, like this woman, have confronted the issues but still seek reassurance.

```
Dear Diane,
    I have questions in regard to what is
a "right" physical relationship between a
```

husband and wife. I am a Christian and so is my husband. However, we believe very differently as to where our physical relationship goes. He has at least dabbled in pornography and had an affair a year and a half ago. We have been getting counseling, but it doesn't seem to be helping in this area.

His belief is that spouses should do whatever their spouse wants them to do—even if it is something they feel extremely uncomfortable doing. My thought is that pressuring your spouse to do things that make them feel degraded is not okay. Those things include oral or anal sex, your spouse wanting you to masturbate so he can watch, or him wanting you to watch "stimulating" movies to "get you going." I have expressed to him that I not only have a conviction about watching these type of movies but that it makes me feel inadequate when he is looking at other bare-breasted women.

I realize this is a very descriptive email, and I'm not even sure it's appropriate to send. However, I'm at my wit's end. My husband continues to tell me what a failure I am and that if I were doing as the Bible says, I would be willing to put my "preferences" aside and do things that fulfill him. I would like to note that I do not, and have never withheld sex from him. I don't believe that I am a "prude," as he has so frequently tried to tell me I am. I am okay with sex. He uses 1 Corinthians as Scripture telling me that my body isn't mine and that I have a duty to him.[1]

Diane's wise response:

Dear . . .

It is sad when the Bible is used as
a weapon rather than a guide to help us
learn how to love and cherish one another
within the marriage. The Scripture your
husband is referring to in 1 Corinthians
asks the husband to "render to his wife
the affection due her" (1 Cor. 7:3 NKJV).
That fits with Ephesians 5:25 that commands
the husband to love his wife as Christ
loves the church. I have found in my own
marriage that because Ted has honored me
in a loving sexual way, it is natural
for me to want to give myself to him. In
fact, we have teased and said to one another, "I am so glad God has given me your
body." This denotes a cherishing rather
than a demanding posture. God's desire as
expressed through Scripture is that we
become intimate allies, and that is only
possible as we deal with the attitudes of
our heart.

You asked what is "right" physically. Ted
and I don't like to dictate what is right
for couples, but these are some guidelines
we have used in our own marriage that have
helped us develop a cherishing attitude
toward one another. If one of us is uncomfortable with trying something, we talk
about it and work it through.

Since oral sex and masturbation are frequent questions and many Christians have
varying views, we have searched Scripture.
The closest the Bible comes to looking at
oral sex is Song of Songs 4:16–5:1 (NKJV),
"Let my beloved come into his garden and
eat its pleasant fruits. . . . I have
come to my garden, . . . I have gathered
my myrrh with my spice; I have eaten my

honeycomb with my honey; I have drunk my wine with my milk." The gardens of spice often refer to the genitals, and many references are made about the oral delights and enjoyment of each other in the Song of Songs.

The Bible does not specifically mention masturbation. Since pornography and masturbation usually go hand in hand, we see this as something that takes away from the intimacy of a couple rather than adding to their discovery and enjoyment of one another.

Some of the other things you listed are not only degrading but can cause contamination. The rectum carries disease-producing microorganisms that can contaminate the urinary bladder and vagina. Contrast that with the genital area that is germ free when washed before intercourse.

So often our society pushes couples toward perversion promising the veneer of excitement. Unfortunately, the poison of pornography and perversion can easily seep in and contaminate the relationship, often causing it to dissolve altogether.

In our seminar we share some healthy tools that can add new excitement to a couple's relationship. These tools help reprogram negative mental pictures from the past. One of these exercises encourages the couple to keep the lights on (even if it is candlelight) and their eyes open during their lovemaking times. It may sound simple, but it isn't. Looking deeply into your spouse's eyes and fully enjoying his or her body, soul, and spirit moves couples to a greater level of intimacy and excitement.

> Finally, I hope you continue with Christian counseling. I know there is a possibility for greater intimacy if you both seek God's best.
>
> Blessings, Diane

I would like to add a few words about the issue of masturbation, which Diane's response mentioned. During the question-and-answer portion of the Sexy Christians Seminar, this issue always comes up. First of all, it is not the unpardonable sin. But a lifestyle characterized by sexual self-gratification leads to a self-focused perspective. I always remember Woody Allen's sardonic comment in the movie *Annie Hall*: "Don't knock masturbation. It's sex with someone I love." When I first heard this, I thought, *What a revealing statement. It* is *all about you.*

Sex with yourself may give you a high, but it's never as fulfilling as the intercourse and intimacy for which God designed us.

Not only is masturbation self-focused, but recent research has shown it is not nearly as satisfying as intercourse. Dr. Stuart Brody discovered the prolactin levels for a climax experienced through intercourse are *four times higher* than for one experienced through masturbation.[2] Prolactin is the hormone that brings us down from an orgasmic high and provides a feeling of satisfaction. Sex with yourself may give you a high, but it's never as fulfilling as the intercourse and intimacy for which God designed us.

Attitude Check

Before we get too upset at that husband's self-centeredness, we should recognize that we all act in self-centered ways at times. We can easily make rude or insensitive comments to our spouse, children, or friends because, in one way or another, each of us is trying to fly with clipped wings.

So what's the answer? A cartoon strip that appeared many years ago aptly illustrates this universal dilemma. The first frame shows the climber braving a high mountain to seek wisdom from an ancient sage. Upon reaching the mountaintop, the climber asks the sage, "What is the key to real happiness?" The sage responds that the key is simple: deprivation, abstinence, poverty, and celibacy. In the final frame the climber does a double-take, looks at the reader, and says, "There has to be somebody else up here I can talk to."

In several decades of counseling couples, I have run into few people who come to me seeking to change themselves instead of their relationship. Their marriage is falling like a rock and they assume they need more power to fix it. They want some quick communication tips and techniques along with easy spiritual solutions. Translation: they want to know how to get their mate to understand them better.

There's one basic problem with this approach: learning how to make *I* versus *you* statements can't and won't fix a marriage. Please don't misunderstand me here. Communication techniques can help, but good techniques alone cannot solve the deeper issues. Since deep inner corrosion has clipped our wings, only inner change can repair the damage.

Most of us want to grow up, but few want the struggle of the growth process. I'm convinced God created marriage to build in us a hunger for real inner growth despite the pain it yields.

The first time I sat in the cockpit of a high-performance aircraft and rocketed into the blue, I was hooked. The first time I connected deeply with Diane, I was hooked even more powerfully. The experience of deep intimacy creates a healthy passion for more. In my relationship with my wife, my quest for further intimacy soon confronted me with the fact that something was broken within me.

I desperately needed God to repair my brokenness, but somehow I had to relax in the process. When you're fighting with God as well as your spouse, nothing seems to work. I had to accept the fact that marriage is more than another flight plan to memorize or checklist to complete.

On my own I could never master the marriage or get everything to work. But by the power of the Holy Spirit I can master *myself* and become comfortable in my own skin. I can discover the person God has uniquely created me to be and hold on to that truth in the turbulent skies of marriage. I can learn how to confront myself when I am getting off course and let God validate me rather than constantly looking to my partner. I can admit when I am wrong and acknowledge my projections and distortions. Above all, I can face the pain involved in growing as a person and as a couple. Instead of beating myself up when I fail and trying harder by applying more power, I can remind myself of God's outrageous, all-encompassing love. Instead of constantly trying to fix my partner, I can let my Father heal my clipped wings by fixing my soul.

The New Testament contains some messages from a top-notch relational flight instructor. His name is James, and he doesn't hesitate to speak his mind. At times his words may seem a bit harsh, but only because we've become accustomed to blaming others for our problems. James doesn't let us delude ourselves. Instead, he points out our clipped wings and helps us understand what we must eliminate if we hope to soar in intimacy:

> Where do you think all these appalling wars and quarrels come from? Do you think they just happen? Think again. They come about because you want your own way, and fight for it deep inside yourselves.
>
> James 4:1–2 Message

James makes it clear. What is the one thing you will never receive? Answer: your own way. And if you want to understand the love of your life, you have to lose *the right to be right*.

Dr. Anthony Wolf, a clinical psychologist, observes that one of the greatest threats to satisfying relationships is "our overwhelming need to be right when we disagree."[3] God has provided the perfect place for couples to experience this truth: the car. Diane has often told me, "The turnoff is back there." To which I respond, "No it isn't; it's up ahead." Then, of course, I keep driving, even if I have to circle the globe to prove I'm right.

When your behavior looks as crazy as that, you know you're flying with clipped wings. James speaks the truth. We must eliminate that "have to be right" attitude or face a relational—especially a marital—crash and burn.

Every time I cite the following statistic in a Sexy Christians Seminar, you can almost hear the stunned silence. Dr. John Gottman of the University of Washington discovered that more than 70 percent of the issues couples argue about will never be resolved.[4] In other words, you can focus on fixing your mate, but that will never fix the problem. You can focus on seeking validation from your partner alone, but that will drive you—and your spouse—crazy. Arguing effectively about an issue has less to do with one person *being* right and much more to do with both partners *feeling* right about the outcome. It may surprise you, but true intimacy does not mean complete agreement between partners on every issue. Instead, it means being healthy and whole enough as a person to be *uncomfortably close* with the person you love.

Lost Leaves

The second thing James helps us see is no less challenging: "When you ask, you do not receive, because you ask with wrong motives, that you may spend what you get on your pleasures" (James 4:3). If you want to understand the love of your life, you need to eliminate the wrong motive of focusing on your pleasure and wanting it all.

Years ago renowned psychologist and theologian Rollo May made a cogent observation about the human condition. He said modern man has taken Adam and Eve's fig leaf, removed it from his genitals, and put it over his face.[5] Our world has effectively turned sex upside down. People are experiencing oneness of the flesh without the oneness of truly loving each other. We now use sex as an attempt to create a depth of relationship that doesn't exist instead of a means to celebrate oneness that does.

God wired us for sexual fulfillment. As Patrick Carnes explained in a lecture for sexual addiction therapists, when we experience sexual arousal and orgasm, our brain floods with feel-good chemicals such as oxytocin, dopamine, adrenaline, endorphins, and serotonin. All of this hits what researchers call the "reward circuit" of the limbic system—the same area of the brain cocaine can trigger. Deep in our memory, this particular area works to intensely underline experiences that trigger great feelings.

To put it simply, God intended sexual intimacy as a healthy high. He designed our brains to bond unforgettably with positive experiences like sex. What does that mean for the average husband or wife? If you walk in true intimacy with your partner, you'll become more deeply bonded to one another after ten, twenty, and thirty years of marriage. You may still be attracted to others, but your partner will increasingly become your sole desire. This explains why God brought one woman—not a harem—to Adam.

Today the fig leaf has not simply moved out of place, it's often out of the picture altogether. People bond to a false image through pornography, especially on the internet. They become attracted and attached to a fantasy world rather than a spouse. This happens not only to men but also to women, who frequently lose the fig leaf too. Recent research reveals 40 percent of women who use the internet engage in problematic cybersex activity.[6]

Once we lose the fig leaf, the high—not the relationship—becomes the focus. That makes intimacy impossible. The next affair, the next internet site, the next marriage, the next steamy romance novel or sexually suggestive chat room becomes the focus. No matter how low we go, we always crave more. That explains why sexual bondage is the strategy from the darkest pits of hell. It promises you everything and leaves you with nothing—every time.

Face It

You're reading this book, so I know you long to understand the love of your life. You want a deeply intimate relationship. Are you ready to change your attitude and understand that you don't always get it right? Are you ready to adjust your motives and learn to put others first?

If you want to become a Sexy Christian, you'll need to follow some further advice from James, who tells us that if we don't get our attitude and motivations right, they will lead to wrong actions: "God gives strength to the humble, but sets himself against the proud and haughty" (James 4:6 TLB). Wrong actions occur when we find ourselves headed away from God. They quickly form a slippery slope from which we can never recover on our own.

But do you know something? Of all the proud and haughty folks I have met, only a few of them genuinely believe they are God's gift to the world. You guessed it: most of them have clipped wings that stem from their deep wounds and disappointments. And many of them act a lot like a friend of mine. Let's call him "Frank." He came to me depressed and discouraged over his marital problems, including the fact that his wife (we'll call her "Lisa") was totally resistant to his sexual advances.

When I talked with Lisa, however, I heard the rest of the story. Frank was going through a very tough time. He had lost his job and couldn't seem to pull himself out of the emotional pit into which he had plunged. Job loss can suck the self-esteem right out of a guy without a close connection to God. Whenever Frank became especially discouraged, he wanted to have sex with his wife. Now they both loved the Lord, so Lisa did not initially resist his advances. Over time, however, she realized that Frank was using their sexual relationship to medicate his pain. The delight he showed immediately after having sex quickly faded into an emotional shutdown; he stopped talking and opening up. Wisely, Lisa became resistant to his sexual advances because he was using sex as a way to guard against vulnerability and intimacy. You see the problem, don't you? Frank had his fig leaf seriously out of place.

When I met with the two together, I sensed that Frank expected me to take his side. After all, Lisa wasn't doing the biblical thing and responding to his sexual needs. She needed a good talking-to, right?

Wrong. I let each of them share about the conflict and then smiled as I looked at Frank. "Fortunately, this stalemate has an easy solution. No sex for you, my friend, until you begin to talk honestly with your wife. She wants real intimacy with you, not just a tussle between the sheets to make you feel good."

I was asking Frank to confront himself. He had to get a grip on who he was and stop trying to fix the marriage. Thankfully, Frank had a great heart for God and recognized the truth of my statements. Humbly, he began to deal with the corrosion underneath his clipped wings.

Here is where things really got interesting. Once Frank opened up, his wife couldn't get enough of him. She wore the guy out! He wasn't depressed anymore—fatigued, sure, but not depressed. Their marriage turned around. Frank's life turned around, and he soon found a great job.

As married couples, we face some storms in life we can only fly through together. First, however, we must face our own issues. As Frank confronted the corrosion within, God began repairing the damaged parts of his past that had kept him earthbound. Soon, he and his bride were able to soar on the wings of the Holy Spirit to depths of intimacy they had never before experienced. Life as a Sexy Christian works. And it shows.

Love Lessons

In order to experience true intimacy, we must confront our inner corrosion.

If we want to experience the rich, powerful sex life God intends for us, something must change. It's not our marriage. It's not our spouse. It's each one of us.

We all have issues that result from past hurts and cause present corrosion. Sometimes the wounds occurred so long ago we don't even remember them. But when we find ourselves angry for no apparent reason, when we insist that we are right in a situation where we're obviously wrong, or when we seek our own way without any thought for the needs of others, those wounds are making their presence known.

Instead of attempting to blame our spouse in order to fix the relationship, *we must first seek to change ourselves.* When we willingly lay down our *right to be right* and allow God to heal the wounds of the past, he can take our marriage to new levels of intimacy. He can make us Sexy Christians.

Home Play

Rules in review: (1) Avoid "you" statements. Instead, talk about your own actions, thoughts, and feelings. (2) Listen. Don't give advice or attempt to psychoanalyze your spouse. (3) If tempers flare, disengage and pray.

1. Think back to your parents' marriage or the marriage of another couple you know well. Did clipped wings have an impact there? If so, how?

2. Ted says on page 130, "When you work on yourself, you're working on your marriage." Do you agree? Why or why not?

3. Use the following checklist to help identify attitudes and behaviors in yourself that may be making marital communication difficult. Ask the Holy Spirit's help to note areas that apply specifically to you and your marriage.

   ☐ Needing to be right
   ☐ Blaming my spouse or circumstances
   ☐ Focusing only on my needs
   ☐ Trying to control or manipulate to get my way
   ☐ Withdrawing physically or emotionally from my spouse
   ☐ Being defensive or making excuses
   ☐ Angry outbursts or responses
   ☐ Other

   _____

4. Discuss with your spouse the areas you have identified separately and confess these areas to God and to one another. Ask the Holy Spirit to replace these negative responses with the fruit of the Spirit: love, joy, peace, patience, kindness, goodness, faithfulness, gentleness, and self-control (Gal. 5:22–23). If possible, pray with your spouse about the changes you each want to make.

Part 3

The Passion

*The Holy Spirit Infuses Our Sexual
Relationship with True Passion as We
Increasingly Surrender Our Lives to the Lord*

9

One Hot Couple

What's the Secret to Great Sex?

TED

One of the things that has always puzzled me is how the church can be so negative toward sex when the Bible is so positive about it. I remember one Sexy Christians Seminar we did at a very conservative church. The pastor unwittingly entered a verbal shooting gallery before the seminar. One gentleman protested the title because it was "too arousing." The pastor asked what was wrong with being aroused with your mate. "Well," the man responded, "I don't like to get that aroused." He must have one exciting marriage, don't you think?

The protesting man is not alone in his struggles. From its earliest days the church has wrestled with the issue of sexuality. Some of the apostolic fathers also took a rather negative view of this topic. Origen, a renowned scholar of the church in the first half of the third century, was so adamant with respect to sexual purity that he castrated himself in response to Matthew 19:12.[1] I'd call this an intense (as well as extremely personal) reaction.

Augustine, the greatest theologian of the early church, declared marriage was acceptable but singleness was preferable. According to his teaching, sexual activity between husband and wife should be allowed only for procreation (producing children). If the couple dared engage in sexual activity for the purpose of enjoyment, they were obviously sinful.[2] From his perspective, Diane and I have been sinning significantly for more than four decades.

Back to the Bible

Fortunately Scripture presents no such outlook. For example, the Old Testament Song of Songs sets forth an exquisite picture of sexual intimacy and love between husband and wife. It depicts in detail the beauty of the sexual relationship in marriage but doesn't mention procreation at all. Instead it focuses completely on the joys and challenges of human sexuality.

I remember my years as a Bible school professor at the undergraduate level. Students often came up to me to ask, "Dr. Roberts, what's the Song of Songs about?"

I smiled because I knew what they meant. They couldn't believe God had such a stunningly positive view of sex. "It's a great book," I told them. "It's the only R-rated book in the Bible. R doesn't stand for raunchy but for outrageously, passionately, Romantic." Then I winked (specifically at the guys) and added, "And the steamiest translation is *The Living Bible*. You need to read it." My last remark certainly boosted Bible sales in our college bookstore.

The depiction of marital intimacy in the Song of Songs is a healthy antidote to the diseased perspective of our day. If you

take time to read the book carefully, you may be taken aback
by the bride's forthrightness. She's not a passive participant or
reflexive responder. Of the book's 119 verses, the bride speaks
in 74 of them, and her words can hardly be called idle chatter.
In the first two chapters alone, she tells her man in a gracious
way exactly how she wants to love him. She also describes how
she wants to be loved in return (Song of Songs 1:2; 2:3, 6). All
this makes for some incredible reading. In today's language,
the Song of Songs is the story of one hot couple!

By the way, Shulamith is every husband's dream bride because she communicates so frankly and erotically. She tells
him precisely how to meet her sexual needs. She gives no
sense of timidity or passivity. She is comfortable in her body
and loves to be loved.

Of course Solomon throws in a few great comments of
his own. He uses poetry and creative expressions to speak
of her beauty and his passion. One verse, though, seemed
like an enigma to me: "Your breasts are like twin fawns of a
gazelle, feeding among the lilies" (Song of Songs 4:5 NLT).
One commentator helped me understand this phrase when
she wrote, "By comparing Shulamith's [the bride] décolletage
to young deer, he's [Solomon] telling her that her breasts look
so soft and sweet he'd really like to pet them!"[3]

This honest, loving expression represents God's view of
sexual relationships between a man and woman who have
committed themselves to walk in his blessings. As you have
begun to understand, God designed marriage as one of his
greatest character-building programs, but he wisely included
a huge element of fun. God placed this and other hot couples
in the Bible as an example of the kind of purpose, power,
and passion real intimacy can bring.

Now that we've settled this issue, what do you think is
God's favorite Bible word about sex? I have asked many folks
this question, and the answer I hear most often is, "No!"
Of course they are speaking in jest, but their words betray
a misconception that God is somehow against sex. I like to

God designed marriage as one of his greatest character-building programs, but he wisely included a huge element of fun.

respond, "You got the answer half right. God's favorite word with respect to sex is k-no-w."

If you look up the word *sex* on your computer (using a Bible software program, not the internet), you'll soon discover the phrase *to know* is most frequently translated to English as *sex*. This is especially true for the Hebrew language. A simple concordance reveals the complexity and depth of the Hebrew word for sexual intercourse, which translates literally as *to know*. Here are just a few of the definitions:

> To observe; to care for; to recognize
> To acknowledge the other person's needs and wants
> To be acquainted with; to instruct; to comprehend
> To be diligent towards; to preserve; to be skillful towards[4]

In other words, God's perspective implies that sex goes far beyond mere genital activity. Instead, your sexuality is directly tied to your life and identity. Did you notice that many of those definitions involve a deep knowing of self that enables you to know someone else intimately? The kind of passion and desire revealed in these words comes from maturation, not infatuation. This is why a healthy, spiritually growing couple has the potential to discover even greater depths of intimacy through the years.

Wired for Intimacy

So if we believe God designed us to be Sexy Christians, what does it take to get there? Scripture distills it down to three important areas covered by the first three sections of this book.

1. Purpose: We spent time discussing the purpose of biblical intimacy in part 1. Since God created us for relationship (with him and with other people), his overall design for sexuality fulfills this purpose.
2. Power: This aspect of our sexuality faces many obstacles, including wounds from the past and present. If we attempt to power up on our own, we face certain destruction. When we deal with issues biblically, however, the power God releases is nothing less than incredible.
3. Passion: We tend to think of passion as a function of biology, but Scripture shows it flows first from an intimate relationship with God. The more we know him, the more we will know our spouse, and the more the passion will flow.

We'll cover the area of passion more completely in the chapters to come. Still, passion's physical aspects have some fascinating roots in God's creation. Let's examine what takes place in the adult brain when we fall in love.

Dr. Helen Fisher conducted some intriguing research on the development of love.[5] Her study discovered gradual changes in brain chemistry that occur over the course of a relationship and lead to diminished passion. Researchers also discovered specific physical phases of "falling in love." In each stage, the couple's brains are saturated with specific neurotransmitters. The levels and types of chemicals change from stage to stage, which has an obvious influence on the way the two feel about each other.

We tend to think of passion as a function of biology, but Scripture shows it flows first from an intimate relationship with God.

The attraction stage: This is the phase of noticing someone, frequently reflecting your specific *arousal template*, which is a mixture of physiology and learning. The arousal template is an unconscious decision tree reflecting how we have been wired sexually. It's also an unconscious guide we use to determine what is arousing or erotic (whether we like tall or short, blondes or redheads, and so forth).

This attraction phase is associated with testosterone, nitric oxide (the same chemical used in Viagra), dopamine, and increasing levels of norepinephrine in the central nervous system. And don't let the medical terminology turn you off, because all this will explain what really turns you on. For example, it is norepinephrine that explains why we can obsess about someone we have just met. Noreprinephine can create an obsessive-compulsive response in which we focus our attention on the positive qualities of the attractive person and overlook or falsely appraise his or her negative traits.

God designed our brains and relationships to move from physical passion to partnership passion, from obsessive love to bonding love.

The romance stage: You may have thought the attraction stage was a bit weird, but in the romance stage we go crazy with love. This is when dopamine rises rapidly and serotonin falls. And increased concentrations of dopamine in the brain are associated with euphoria, hyperactivity, increased mental activity, and decreased need for sleep.[6] In other words, the rising levels of dopamine can make us act like a dope. We throw caution completely out the window. We're in love!

Fortunately, scientists have discovered that within six to eighteen months our brains regain their neurochemical balance. God didn't design us to seek passion as our ultimate goal. And as we have already seen, true biblical intimacy goes much deeper than the initial neurotransmitter rush.

The commitment stage: This stage is associated with the chemical oxytocin in women and vasopressin in men. These neurotransmitters are essential to a sense of security and bonding in a long-term relationship. God designed our brains and relationships to move from physical passion to partnership passion, from obsessive love to bonding love.

Layered Look

The implications of these neurochemical findings extend well past the physical realm, which is illustrated below.

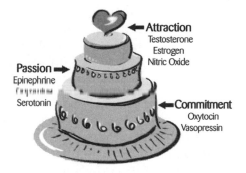

Have you ever seen a one-layer wedding cake? Of course not. But in today's world many people mistakenly seek out a one-layer relationship. Often they end up moving from one quick pairing to another. Frequently people like this are using the *rush* of the initial attraction to medicate some deep pain within. Men can become addicted to lust (initial attraction), which is why pornography becomes a swirling black hole that pulls them in. Women can become addicted to a romantic high through avenues that include multiple relationships, pornographic chat rooms, or steamy romance novels.

What's the problem? One-layer people seek the initial jolt of the neurotransmitters. When this rush begins to fade, they think it's time to find another relationship. Sexual addicts are men and women who have become caught in the neural pathways of a destructive cycle. They are using the high of attraction and romance to medicate their inner woundedness. In today's world the rush can even be generated by the pseudo-high of the internet. The digital replaces the real, which results in an escalation of destruction because people who seek internet satisfaction quickly lose the ability to make human connections. Compulsion is the core of the addictive process, and it relies on these neural pathways of the brain.[7]

Here's the good news. In a long-term, healthy relationship a couple can experience the deep, evocative hues and textures of sincere commitment. As their level of intimacy deepens, they discover attraction and romance in an entirely new way. Unlike what many self-help books teach, real intimacy is more than mere self-disclosure. It's a twofold process: first you confront yourself, and then you self-disclose to your partner. I can disclose the familiar, comfortable parts of myself to my mate, but that won't create a profound sense of intimacy. *The real electricity and passion occurs when I confront myself and grow as a person in Christ.*

Suddenly my spouse has an entirely new dimension of my life to discover. This fresh attraction can move the relationship further into intimacy. When we share the multilayered process and experience growth that continues throughout our years of life together, we become one hot couple!

Death by Marriage

As I pointed out in chapter 3, marriage may initially feel as though God designed it to crucify you. And in one sense he did exactly that. He created it to expose our self-centeredness as nothing else can. He ingeniously set marriage up to push us toward self-confrontation in areas of our life to which we have remained blind.

But instead, we can easily (and wrongly) turn from self-confrontation to mate-confrontation. One man expressed a common reaction when he declared, "My wife went from hard to get, to hard to handle, to hard to take." This man is burying himself by his reactions to his wife. The resurrection of the dream God gave them when they walked down the aisle will never occur until he begins the process of self-confrontation.

Sometimes we won't feel supported or validated by our mate. That's part of the death process. We've already begun to examine openness and understanding along with their relationship to marital intimacy. But since these two elements are so critical, why do we find it so difficult to incorporate them into our relationship? Why do we struggle so much to be open and understanding with the person we love the most? Why do those wounds and family patterns of the past rise up and make openness such an excruciating choice? Let's explore a little more.

In the early years of our marriage, I consistently failed to include openness in my marital flight plan. Out of her frustration with my attitude, Diane would say things like, "Come on, Ted, open up. Tell me what's really going on inside you."

Those words literally sent a shiver down my spine. I froze on the inside, but I covered my inner turmoil with an outer expression of anger. I was suffering—and making my wife suffer—from my clipped wings because I hadn't yet confronted the issues of my past. We had the potential to be one hot couple, but the thermostat of our marriage was stuck in the "Off" position.

Previously we discussed the significant impact the portion of your brain known as the *amygdala* can have on your actions. (Remember the male teenager's mental sexual prompt every fifty-two seconds?) But the amygdala deals with more than mere sexual desire. It belongs to the larger limbic system that functions as a deep memory structure. The amygdala tags or colors various events from your past as either safe or dangerous.[8] It acts as an internal highlighter to help code your memories.

In my dysfunctional family system, I learned at an early age that if I expressed my personal needs, bad things would happen. I can still remember the day in first grade when I got hurt while playing outside and asked one of my stepfathers (I eventually had seven) to help me. He slapped me on the side of the head and told me to toughen up.

That kind of threatening environment trains you early on to find a system—any system—for survival. My inner mantra became, "Don't be vulnerable; you can make it on your own." And in my family of origin, that choice made sense. It certainly reduced the number of painful personal conflicts I had to endure.

Because of this choice, however, my short-term solution gradually became a long-term problem. Once the limbic system is programmed, it responds automatically and subconsciously whenever something triggers it. When vulnerability issues occur, the limbic system will automatically kick in. When I was in first grade, my inner programming helped me survive. But before I knew it, twenty years had passed and that same reaction threatened to kill my marriage. The insecure response of my inner programming manifested itself in an attempt to control.

Angry on the outside, withdrawn on the inside—you can imagine what this did to our level of marital intimacy. This loss, like every loss of intimacy, leads to an increase in isolation and self-gratification. I found myself deeply wounding the woman I loved through my crazy (and at the time, incomprehensible) reactions.

Breaking Point

One day I came to an important decision. I stopped blaming Diane for the problem. I realized change begins with awareness and awareness brings responsibility. I had to confront myself and my feelings, but I didn't have a clue how to do it. I desperately wanted to have a fulfilling marriage, deep intimacy, and a mutually fulfilling sex life, but I was killing my dream with the destructive weapon of my actions. I withdrew from my wife and became angry at her for the pressure she placed on me to "open up." And I fed my anger by constantly blaming her for the problem. Yet beneath it all lay my deep fear of being vulnerable or showing a hint of weakness. How could Diane and I experience the resurrection of our dreams together? How can you?

After decades of counseling fellow strugglers, I've made an amazing discovery: Since destructive patterns frequently operate at the instinctive or limbic level, the solution is not more information. Instinct always trumps information. I had enough information to realize I should open up to my wife, but I had too many limbic alarms going off in my brain to take this important step.

King David and his son Solomon (who wrote the Song of Songs) illustrate this problem perfectly. As I pointed out in the first part of this chapter, Solomon showed extraordinary insight into romantic love. He had also seen the devastating implosion of his father's life through his sexual sin with Bathsheba. Yet Solomon, known as the wisest man in the world, ended up with seven hundred wives and three hundred concubines (1 Kings 11:3).

Solomon's stupidity defies description. He had to remember an average of two wedding anniversaries every day and ended up with not one, not two, but seven hundred mothers-in-law! Obviously the boy was brain-dead. He was trying to nourish himself with seven hundred one-layer wedding cakes without ever reaching the deeper layers of commitment and intimacy. And if you read the final book he wrote in the Bible, Ecclesiastes, you'll see how bad things eventually got.

I remember thinking at my lowest point, *Lord, is there any hope for me? Will I ever break this destructive pattern?* That marked my breaking point because the beginning of *healing* is *feeling*. I needed to feel the pain I was causing my mate and come to grips with the pain I had carried inside myself for years. The pattern I was struggling with in my heart had been programmed through painful experiences. It could only be reprogrammed through new and healthy experiences in the same area as my wounding.

You see, the limbic system does not respond to mere information. It responds to experiences. No, I did not even remotely comprehend this at the time of my struggle, but somehow my soul did. As I cried out to Father God, he responded to me in a way that changed everything.

What's Next, Papa?

Still an active member of the military, I prepared for another evening flight. As I prayed over the night's work, my heart was heavy over a recent disagreement with Diane. I read a few chapters in Romans, and Paul's words rolled around in my soul: "This resurrection life you received from God is not a timid, grave-tending life. It's adventurously expectant, greeting God with a childlike 'What's next, Papa?'" (Rom. 8:15 Message).

After reading this verse, I closed my eyes. Tears spontaneously streamed down my face. With the inner eyes of my spirit, I saw an enormous pants leg standing before me. Somehow I understood; I was beholding the presence of Father God. As if by instinct, I reached over to hug the leg, realizing I finally had a Papa who would always be there for me.

Previously I thought folks who saw spiritual visions had only one oar in the water. But the pants-leg experience changed my life. It released me from the grave-tending, self-protecting patterns I had learned as a kid. Father God was calling me into adventure! I was a child again, but a child with a dad I could trust, a dad who loved me enough to take care of me forever. God's goodness was reprogramming the depths of my heart and mind. It would have taken years for me to work out what took place in a moment in the presence of my Father God. Finally I was able not only to *react* to my wife's words or actions but to *respond* to her as a person of infinite value. I could do the right thing. Yes, the right thing is always the hard thing, but soul-fulfilling intimacy with your mate is worth any price.

That day our marriage began a journey toward deep intimacy and our sexual relationship started to turn around. I pray you too will move ever deeper into one another's hearts as a couple. I pray you will leave behind the painful, repetitive patterns of the past and discover instead the passionate patterns of your gracious heavenly Father. I pray you too will become Sexy Christians.

Love Lessons

God designed us for intimate relationships.

From the smallest neurochemical reaction to the most passionate emotional response, God has wired us for intimacy. Although specific processes and patterns play a large part in the attraction process, true intimacy results from deep growth within the relationship (maturation) rather than mere biological or genital drives (infatuation). When we live with integrity and nurture relationships that honor his creation by reflecting intimacy as he designed it, we demonstrate the Sexy Christians lifestyle God wants us to have.

The key to breaking destructive patterns is an intimate relationship with our Father God.

Our limbic system—the brain's storage area for memory patterns—responds to experiences rather than information. When we surrender the deepest parts of ourselves to our heavenly Father, he reprograms destructive patterns and overcomes any evil found there. We can move toward deep intimacy in our marriage relationships when we embrace his incredible love for us as his children.

Home Play

Rules in review: (1) Avoid "you" statements. Instead, talk about your own actions, thoughts, and feelings. (2) Listen. Don't give advice or attempt to psychoanalyze your spouse. (3) If tempers flare, disengage and pray.

1. In the first part of this chapter Ted discussed the fact that individuals and churches sometimes hold a negative view of sex. Rate the level of approval about discussion or teaching on sex by the groups mentioned below (1 low, 5 high).

   a. My family of origin   1 2 3 4 5
   b. The first church to which I belonged   1 2 3 4 5
   c. My college or university   1 2 3 4 5
   d. My church today   1 2 3 4 5
   e. Jesus Christ   1 2 3 4 5

2. "Passion . . . comes from maturation, not infatuation." Write a few sentences to explain why you agree or disagree with Ted's statement.

3. As a boy Ted decided that in order to survive in his dysfunctional family, he had to avoid vulnerability. Think back to your childhood and a time when openness or vulnerability hurt you. Share the story with your spouse.

4. Take turns reading the following Scriptures aloud: Psalm 139; Romans 8:31–38; 1 John 3:1–3. Then pray together and ask God to reveal himself to you as Papa.

10

One Cold Bed

How Does Real Intimacy Work?

TED AND DIANE

One year Diane and I managed to get away for a New Year's vacation. Our beautiful state of Oregon had been particularly cold and wet during December, so we had a great time thawing out for a few days in a warmer climate. But vacations don't last forever. The time came when we had to face life's (literally) cold realities once again.

We arrived home at one o'clock in the morning, desperately in need of sleep. Since we had turned off the heat in our house more than a week before, it was cold! We stood silently beside our bed. Neither of us wanted to jump under the covers. In fact, the white sheets were so chilly they looked blue. Diane stood in her flannel pajamas and fluffy slippers watching me. Finally she burst out, "I am not getting in that bed until you hop in and warm up my side!"

I was stunned but silent. Inside my head, though, the words tumbled out: *I can't believe she actually said that. You know, single guys would never believe stuff like this actually happens in a marriage. Of course, if they did, they probably wouldn't get married at all.*

True biblical intimacy is never easy, especially in a cold bed. Diane had clearly made her needs known. How would I respond?

Let me ask you an interesting question: Within the context of your marriage, what are your top three sex needs? Take time to write them down now. Go ahead; put the book down. Write out your top three needs and have your spouse do the same. Instead of sharing your responses with one another immediately, though, wait until the Home Play exercise at the end of this chapter.

In my decades of pastoral ministry, I've spoken with hundreds of men about their sexual needs. Consistently I've found that their needs encompass three primary areas. Recent research backs up the conclusions I've drawn by listening to men's hearts.

First, men want to experience *mutual fulfillment*. Granted, a newlywed or a man who is emotionally unstable may not consider this important. Over time, however, husbands who have a genuine heart for God discover the ability to see beyond themselves and their own sexual needs. They want their wives to be fulfilled too, which makes mutual feedback necessary. If we want to experience deep intimacy, we must start talking to one another about sex.

Second, men deeply desire *connection with their wives*. Yes, this provides a sharp contrast to all the beer commercials and other stereotypical presentations of males in modern media. Still, deep in their hearts, most husbands want to experience the emotional richness of intimacy.

So what's the problem? One sentence: the typical husband attempts to connect physically before he connects emotionally. Women look for the emotional connection first. Although they both have the same goal in mind, the husband's approach is vastly different from his wife's. And this can cause the kind of pain and problems that move couples away from intimacy every time.

The third sexual need among men is their desire for a "Song of Songs" wife. To tell the truth, I've never actually heard a man express it this way, but the moment I use the phrase they immediately say, "Yes. That's exactly what I mean."

A Song of Songs wife is a woman who is comfortable with her body and her sexuality. She enjoys being the initiator at times. She delights in sex and looks forward to being intimate with her husband. In other words, a Song of Songs wife is a Sexy Christian.

Some Like It Hot

After Ted's comments at the beginning of the chapter, my insistence that he warm up the bed may seem like cruel and unusual punishment. But here's the rest of the story.

Throughout our more than forty years of marriage, Ted has commented on the difference in our personal thermostats. He likes it cold; I like it hot. In order to emphasize this distinction (especially when it comes to the bedroom), he likes to say, "I like the windows open with a cold breeze blowing through and icicles hanging from my toes."

We thought an electric blanket with two sets of controls, one for each person, would solve this minor marital conflict. It did until one eventful night. Earlier in the day we had flipped our mattress and unknowingly switched the blanket's controls. I couldn't figure out why I was freezing, so I turned up my side (or what I thought was my side) as high as it would go. Ted soon became so hot he turned what he thought was his side of the blanket off completely.

In the morning the battle wounds became evident: frostbite for me, legs covered with burn marks for Ted. That was the end of the electric blanket. In its place Ted promised to be "all the heat" I'd need. Hence my request that he warm up my side of the bed.

Temperatures aside, here are the top three sexual needs expressed by women. The first is the need for *affirmation*. A woman longs to receive verbal comments that emphasize and reemphasize her husband's love. She needs to know he finds her attractive. Statistics show four out of five women acknowledge they sometimes feel insecure about their husband's love.[1] Some obvious factors including infidelity or physical violence can yield this kind of marital insecurity. Other more subtle factors include unresolved conflict, a husband who routinely withdraws into his man-cave, or the silent treatment. Any of these responses can prompt her to wonder inwardly: *Does he really love me?*

Thanks especially to Hollywood's continual barrage of *ideal* faces and figures, nearly all women struggle with body image. This battle goes back to biblical times. In the first chapter of the Song of Songs, Shulamith shows concern because she—a country girl with dark skin—bears little resemblance to the city girls who have previously surrounded her betrothed. Wisely, Solomon understands a woman's need for affirmation. He continually speaks words to her that emphasize her beauty. When a man stays tuned in to his wife's need for affirmation, he gives her a wonderful gift: the gift of feeling secure in their relationship.

Husbands and wives have the same number two need: *connection*. Unlike men, however, whose primary focus is physical connection, women desire verbal, emotional, and spiritual connection. I am a night owl by nature and Ted is an early bird, but long ago we made a commitment to go to bed at the same time. Over the years this has required some negotiation, but it allows us to pray together each night and have times of physical intimacy. I believe this simple commitment has helped us achieve the connection we both crave.

Women's third sexual need is *nonsexual touch*. Ted likes to ask, jokingly, if such a thing exists, but he knows better. A morning good-bye kiss, moments spent cuddling while watching the news, or back and foot rubs all help create the closeness a woman desires. If every touch has a sexual agenda, a woman feels devalued. Before long she may become cynical and shy away from any kind of touch.

God has built a longing deep in the heart of every woman, a desire to be treasured for who she is—body, soul, and spirit. Nonsexual touch tells her, "I love and cherish all of you and want to feel close to you even without making love."[2]

Relational Intimacy

It should be apparent by now that sexual fulfillment is a multi-faceted challenge. Deep inside, though, men and women seek exactly the same thing. Dr. John Gottman made an illuminating comment about the similarity of our deepest desires as husband and wife: "The determining factor in whether wives feel satisfied with the sex, romance and passion in their marriage is by 70 percent the quality of the couple's friendship. For men, the determining factor is by 70 percent the quality of the couple's friendship. So men and women come from the same planet after all!"[3]

This underlines why the biological drive model of human sexuality cannot adequately explain the dynamics of our most intimate relationships. Our neocortex (the higher reasoning part of our brain) gives us the ability to control our impulses.[4] If we didn't have this ability, God would never challenge us (as he does in his Word) to walk in sexual holiness. In other words, we are not animals who simply experience sexual feelings and respond. We have the ability to interpret these feelings and decide on a course of action. In fact, how you feel about sexual sensations and receive them has a more significant impact on you than the sensations themselves. Perceived feelings have a stronger impact on your sexual function and orgasm than the physical sensations ever will.[5]

That explains why what we call the *friendship factor* plays such a huge part in intimacy. For example, you may choose to learn a new physical technique in an effort to strengthen your sexual relationship. Although this may help in some ways, it will never take the place of an honest examination of the interplay between you and your mate.

Intimacy is at least a four-dimensional reality. We have already discussed the *physical* and *emotional* aspects of intimacy. We are continuing with the *relational* dimension, followed by the *spiritual*.

Doesn't *relational intimacy* sound like the ultimate redundancy? It's amazing, though, how many couples have never stopped to think about the various aspects of relational intimacy. The first two reveal our uniquely male and female approaches. Women tend to value verbal intimacy, and men have a high need for recreational intimacy.

Regardless of what you may have learned, proper verbal communication is not an instant cure-all for marital intimacy problems, especially if you don't like the message(s) your spouse sends. Yes, the ability to communicate non-accusatory verbal messages (including *I* instead of *you* statements) helps a relationship flourish. The theory that these verbal skills will eventually lead to true intimacy, however, is simply not true. Dr. Gottman's research confirms this fact.

After studying 650 couples and tracking the fate of their marriages for up to fourteen years, we now understand that the active listening technique in counseling couples doesn't work—not just because it is nearly impossible for most couples to do well, but more importantly because successful conflict resolution isn't what makes marriage succeed.[6]

Some folks find this final comment a bit startling because they don't understand the fiery realities of intimacy. The issue centers around a single question: What do you do when your spouse understands your message but totally disagrees with you? Paradoxically, *intimacy actually comes—even grows—through conflict, disagreement, self-confrontation, and self-affirmation in Christ.* These interpersonal skills allow your relationship to move toward a passionate intimacy that could not exist without the sharpening effect of conflict. And if the two of you have a strong sense of recreational intimacy, you'll be equipped to douse any verbal fires that threaten your relationship.

Intimacy actually comes—even grows—through conflict, disagreement, self-confrontation, and self-affirmation in Christ.

To build a healthy relationship with your spouse, it is crucial that you find something fun you love to do together. I admit Diane and I have struggled with this aspect of our marriage because God has designed us so differently. I love to work out until I pass out. If Diane breaks a sweat, she considers it the unpardonable sin. I love to scuba dive. Diane prefers to sit on the beach and soak up the sun. You get the picture.

It took a while, but we finally discovered something we love to do together: ride a motorcycle. When I ride, it's much safer to have her along because I tend to put the pedal down a little too hard. Diane and I have a wonderful system set up to cover this issue. If I exceed the speed limit the slightest bit, she taps the back of my helmet. I've learned to agree with her definition of safety so we can enjoy our rides.

Spiritual Intimacy

In today's world the spiritual aspect of intimacy is the one couples miss most often. It is also the most profound dimension of the entire sexual experience. Otherwise Paul never would have referred to the union between husband and wife as a metaphor for Christ and the church (Eph. 5:23).

Diane and I have led hundreds of seminars about sexual intimacy. In the process we've found far too many husbands and wives who are bored and frustrated with their sex lives. These couples have made the painful discovery that merely experiencing orgasm together does not satisfy the deep needs of the soul.

Great sex is not reserved for the tight-body types who master all the latest kinky sex positions. Instead it is the domain of those who really know themselves, their spouse, and their God.

If you want to have a fulfilling, satisfying sex life that grows through the years, mutual spiritual growth is not optional. Great sex is not reserved for the tight-body types who master all the latest kinky sex positions. Instead it is the domain of those who really know themselves, their spouse, and their God.

Remember, great sex comes from a great heart. It involves an experience of the eternal that transcends our natural self-centeredness and moves us to lose ourselves in the depths of a relationship with our spouse and our God.

You and your spouse need to dream together. When you dream the dreams God has for your marriage, incredible things can take place. That's why praying together is so crucial—not as a religious activity but as a relational one. When you are headed in the same direction in Christ, you can pass through the rivers, mountains, and valleys together. And nothing brings about self-affirmation and self-confrontation like walking in unity within the vision God has for you.

Yes, God has dreams for you as individuals, but he also has a dream for you as a couple. That's why he brought you together. The two of you have far more potential and far more at stake than paying the bills, raising the kids, paying off the mortgage, and being put in a hole in the ground one day. God brought you together to impact your world for his glory and his kingdom. As an expression of the relationship between two of his chosen children who are loved with an outrageous, everlasting love, your sexual intimacy should never become boring or routine.

By now an obvious question comes to mind: If husbands and wives basically desire the same thing from their relationship, and if we realize intimacy is spiritual at its core, why do we find it so difficult? The answer: because intimacy is spiritual at its core.

Stick with me. You can't understand intimacy without grasping some basic theological facts. The *cold bed* arguments go all the way back to primordial days. The third chapter of Genesis tells us that everything changed when Adam and Eve decided to do their own thing. God describes exactly what they brought on themselves:

> To the woman he said, "I will greatly increase your pains in childbearing; with pain you will give birth to children. Your desire will be for your husband, and he will rule over you."
>
> Genesis 3:16

> To Adam he said, . . . "Cursed is the ground because of you; through painful toil you will eat of it all the days of your life."
>
> Genesis 3:17

The word *desire* in God's verdict for Eve conveys not romance but frustration. And the fact that Adam will *rule over* the relationship means that from this point forward intimacy will become a continual challenge. The first couple—and every other couple to come—struggled with a deep sense of isolation from God that profoundly undermined their relationship with one another.

The bottom line: *pain is part of living in a fallen world.* Every human being faces the dilemma of what to do with the pain that comes with life. Along with great joy, some of the deepest pain we ever experience flows from our closest relationships.

Got Pain?

The question of what to do with our pain is, in fact, a central theme of the Bible itself. In the Old Testament, the book of Job is unique. It is not written by a Jew, nor does it deal with the history of Israel. Instead it focuses on some of the basic struggles of humankind throughout history. Job, a successful husband, father, and businessman, suddenly loses everything: home, wealth, health, children—everything. In an instant he goes from the top of the Fortune 500 to total destitution. He finds himself in the land of Uz—a place where pain comes without warning or explanation and leaves its victims like flotsam in a whirlpool of chaos. The third chapter of Genesis tells us we all will spend some time in the land of Uz.

I used to think the main point of the book of Job is the question, "Where is God when I hurt?" This seemed like the main question in my life when I was wrestling with pain. But I came to see the bigger, more fundamental question is the one Satan asks God: "Does Job fear God for nothing?" (Job 1:9). Our adversary declares through his rhetorical question that we only serve God for what we can get out of him. Satan wants us to believe that in a dog-eat-dog world the idea of intimacy with a gracious and loving God is a farce. The world teaches us to put ourselves first and to look out for number one because no one else will. Every couple who buys into this worldview, however, will fail to experience the depth of intimacy God designed for us.

Is my pain meaningless? The question haunts us all when we find ourselves in the land of Uz. If we fail to find the meaning in our pain, we will almost certainly give up on the relationship, whether it's a friendship, a marriage, or our relationship with God.

No Offense

Job isn't the only biblical figure who struggles with this question. John the Baptist, a man identified by Jesus as the greatest of the Old Testament–style prophets, finds himself in jail facing execution. He sends several messengers to Jesus to ask if he is the Messiah. On the surface it sounds like a strange question; God had already revealed this truth to John. In fact, John had publicly declared it to anyone who would listen. So what caused his concern? You see it in Jesus's response:

> Jesus answered and said to them, "Go and report to John what you hear and see: the blind receive sight and the lame walk, the lepers are cleansed and the deaf hear, the dead are raised up, and the poor have the gospel preached to them. And blessed is he who does not take offense at Me."
>
> Matthew 11:4–6 NASB

Like Job, John the Baptist struggles in his relationship with God. John knows that part of Jesus's prophesied (and later self-proclaimed) job description is to set prisoners free. Yet at the time of his questions, John is sitting in a jail cell waiting to lose his head.

John struggles not to take offense; Job struggles not to take offense. Most of us would say Job had good reason to be upset. I would call losing your job, your children, your property, and your health a major cause of offense, wouldn't you? In most of his book, Job pours out his heart to God about the terrible things that have happened in his life. Of course Job is not alone in his struggles with God, which is precisely why Jesus points out to John, "Blessed is he who does not take offense at me" (v. 6).

Taking offense at God makes us bitter. When we become bitter, self-preservation directs our lives. At that point our ability to be intimate with God fades like a morning mist in the rising heat of our frantic efforts and frustrations.

Let's take it deeper. Soon Herod does the unthinkable and has John beheaded. When Jesus hears of the demeaning end to this exemplary life, the Bible says he goes away alone in a boat to a solitary place (Matt. 14:13). Scripture doesn't tell us what he was thinking, but it was obviously intense. I believe he was struggling with the fact that his own cousin had died for him. Of course, as the Son of God, Jesus knew he would one day die for the sins of all humankind, but I believe the loss of John puzzled his humanity. He knew he had the power to set prisoners free. He only did what his Father led him to do, though, and God the Father never directed him to free John. That's why he had to spend time alone with his Father. He needed to renew their intimate relationship.

The God Connection

At times we must relinquish our demand to understand in order to receive the peace that goes beyond understanding. If we don't allow our faith to surpass our comprehension, we'll never get the peace we need. As we allow God to lead us past what we know, he draws us into an understanding that far surpasses our own. And at that point, we reach new depths of intimacy with him.

How much does this have to do with our intimacy as husband and wife? Everything. If you keep demanding that your spouse accept your definition of reality, you'll keep getting the same results: emotional death on the installment plan. That's why couples who have been married for years can sit in a romantic restaurant and barely speak to one another. They've heard it all, and they'd rather not hear it one more time. They've become offended. The battle lines have been drawn and the relationship has moved into trench warfare. The truth is, offended people don't want to take steps toward renewed intimacy because they're afraid they'll lose control of the outcome.

If we don't allow our faith to surpass our comprehension, we'll never get the peace we need.

Do you see why a vibrant relationship with God enables you to experience deep intimacy with your spouse? Being intimate with God—especially through the tough times when he does things you can't understand—helps you learn to relinquish control. You stop being offended by God because every now and then he does something that amazes you. Initially his actions may seem straight out of Uz. Like Job, however, as you hold on and stay intimately connected to God you will find yourself saying, "But as for me, I know that my Redeemer lives, and that he will stand upon the earth at last" (Job 19:25 NLT).

And now for the bottom line: *I have never met a couple with a deep, intimate relationship with God who didn't also have a growing, intimate relationship with each other.* We'll go through more specific elements of the challenge of intimacy in the next chapter, but without the foundation of an intimate relationship with God it's nearly impossible to accomplish. That's why true followers of Christ have a unique advantage in developing a deep connectedness in their marriage.

You may be saying, "Sure, I'd like to connect with God in a deeper way, but I don't have a clue how to do it." We get it backwards. We tend to think of it as our job to connect with

God. If the connection depends on me, though, it produces anxiety rather than peace.

It reminds me of my college years. I enjoyed dating, but I absolutely hated the risk involved in making the call or asking the question. Beneath my youthful bravado and swagger, I was anxious about being rejected. Having endured seven stepfathers, rejection had become part of both my lifestyle and my underlying mental framework.

You may have had a less dysfunctional family background, but I can almost guarantee you have a place somewhere in your soul that reacts to the potential of rejection. When the idea that I must initiate a relationship with God takes root in my mind, I become endangered. Why? Because at either the conscious or unconscious level, I believe rejection is possible. This sets me up for a deadly cycle of religious performance. In other words, I must get God to like me so I can have a relationship with him.

So where should you begin instead? Try this truth: *God passionately wants a relationship with you.* He desires it so intensely that he sent his only Son to die for the wrong things you've done. I can't imagine allowing my son to die for anyone. But that's the point after all; God's love is literally beyond our ability to comprehend. You never have to fear that God doesn't want you or will reject you. He can't do it because he loves you outrageously, amazingly, and eternally.

How many times have I listened to someone delineate the reasons God should reject him or her, all based on actions from the past? People who think like this have disqualified themselves. And how many husbands have told me (in one way or another) they don't feel spiritual enough to draw close to their wives? These thoughts are always lies because the devil is a liar and always has been. Christ, however, loves you so much that he crawled into the cold sheets of death and hell. He brought the warmth of life—eternal life—to you. And this means you can be so committed to intimacy with your spouse you'll warm her side of the bed at one o'clock in the morning.

Love Lessons

True intimacy is both complicated and simple.

Numerous factors affect marital intimacy. Men and women have different sexual needs and express them in different ways. Yet both genders value connectedness and the communication that goes along with it. The friendship factor—the relationship between the husband and wife—is the overriding factor that determines a couple's satisfaction with their marriage. True biblical intimacy is verbal, physical, relational, and especially spiritual in nature.

Because people have the ability to process rather than simply act on our feelings or emotions, we can make wise choices that put our partner first. When we exhibit Christlike willingness to lay down the right to have our own needs met and choose to put our partner's needs above our own, we're on our way to achieving true biblical intimacy.

A vibrant relationship with God makes intimacy work.

Intimacy with God makes a great training and proving ground for an intimate relationship with your spouse. As you trust God and walk with him through times of joy and sorrow, pleasure and pain, you learn to relinquish control. As you uncurl your clenched fist and release the big areas of your life to him, he reminds you that he—not you—holds it all.

Many husbands and wives live in a constant state of being offended—sometimes with each other and sometimes with God himself. If we want to achieve true peace, we must relinquish our *demand to understand* and accept the things God brings into our lives, including his outrageous, overwhelming love. A growing, intimate relationship with God on the part of both spouses is the best predictor of a growing, intimate marriage relationship.

Home Play

Rules in review: (1) Avoid "you" statements. Instead, talk about your own actions, thoughts, and feelings. (2) Listen. Don't give advice or attempt to psychoanalyze your spouse. (3) If tempers flare, disengage and pray.

1. Name an area of your marriage in which (like temperature preferences for Ted and Diane) your needs seem completely opposite from your partner's. Share with your spouse if appropriate for your situation.

2. In case you didn't write down your top sexual needs as Ted asked you to do in this chapter, here's another chance. On a scale of 1–5 (1, not a need at all; 5, a high need), circle how important you consider each need to be.

   a. verbal communication   1 2 3 4 5
   b. physical intimacy   1 2 3 4 5
   c. relational intimacy   1 2 3 4 5
   d. spiritual intimacy   1 2 3 4 5

3. Think back to a specific time or incident when your partner willingly laid down his or her rights in order to meet your needs. Write a few words to describe that loving expression here. Then spend time sharing and thanking one another.

4. Rate the spiritual temperature of your marriage on the following thermometer scale. Discuss with one another what you think might need to change and why.

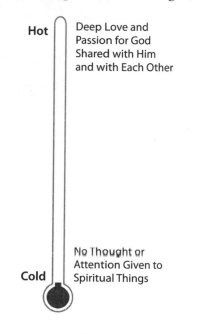

Hot — Deep Love and Passion for God Shared with Him and with Each Other

Cold — No Thought or Attention Given to Spiritual Things

11

Fire-Starters

How Can I Kindle the Flame of Passion?

DIANE

Not long ago Ted and I were leading an out-of-town seminar and I needed an item from a department store. As I stood in line to pay the clerk, I mentioned how glad I was they carried exactly what I needed for the seminar. The clerk asked what kind of seminar I meant, and I responded, "A Sexy Christians Seminar."

She looked a little shocked, even perplexed, but two women in their early eighties standing right behind me quickly responded, "It's so great that you're talking about sex." The older of the two shared that her husband recently passed away and she really missed the "great sex" they had right up until the end of his life. She went on to explain that a few years before her husband's death she asked her doctor if he thought it was okay for them to remain sexually active this late in life. The doctor looked at her with a big smile on his face and said, "Absolutely. Now I have something to look forward to."

No wonder Ted likes to tell couples, "The best years of sex are ahead of you. A couple in their twenties can't compete with a couple in their fifties or even their late seventies when it comes to intimacy." Sex is a very intimate act, but as we have already learned, real intimacy is a by-product of a healthy relationship. One of the best definitions of intimacy I've found says: *Real intimacy is relating rightly to another person [and God] with vulnerability, transparency, caring, acceptance, and commitment.* This means real intimacy is, as we said earlier, being willing to be uncomfortably close with the person you love. In a nutshell, *true intimacy is a by-product of my shared life with Christ and a transparent life with my spouse.*[1]

> *In a nutshell, true intimacy is a by-product of my shared life with Christ and a transparent life with my spouse.*

Fanning the Flame

People love to ask Ted and me about passion. They often wonder how we keep the sexual fires burning after more than forty years of marriage. We tell them great sex always starts with great hearts: first, the heart of God, who longs to bring his life into every part of the marriage; and second, the hearts of partners who allow God to change them from the inside out. Both kindle the sparks of passion, and from there, the flame of intimacy grows.

In the previous chapters, we emphasized personal change. We also discussed ways to confront and eliminate intimacy-breaking factors from the lives of the individual partners. As we began our chapters on passion, we discussed the biological blessings and barriers of God's design for marital intimacy. We talked about choices you can make as an individual that will help move you toward intimacy with God and with your spouse. But by now you may be wondering when we'll return to challenges you can tackle as a couple. Are there things you can do or say together to enhance your relationship?

Of course!

We've already mentioned the vital role trust plays in a marriage relationship. Partners who allow God's Holy Spirit to help them confront wounds from the past and other pain-producing issues find fresh trust beginning to grow. As we've seen, trust fans the flame of intimacy. But how do you keep that flame alive? The answer lies in the same two words we've used before: *openness* and *understanding*.

The figure below shows the connection between openness (transparency and vulnerability) and understanding (caring and acceptance). The more the two overlap, the more a couple will experience genuine intimacy. Great sex—not to mention incredible passion—comes from a great heart.

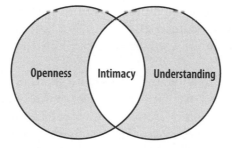

As a young married couple, neither Ted nor I had any understanding of true intimacy. Ted has already shared that he came from an alcoholic home with multiple stepdads. In previous chapters you have seen how the Holy Spirit began a transforming work in his heart when he committed his life to Christ. Although I was a Christian when we married, it took me years to see the areas of my life Christ wanted to change. Most of my dysfunctions were a little more socially acceptable than Ted's and therefore took me longer to recognize.

Although my parents had Christian values and were married almost fifty years before my mom died, God gradually opened my eyes to the fact that I had dragged some unhealthy family patterns into our marriage. Because I was a perfectionist, I believed I must perform in order to earn the approval of others. I also grew up believing good girls don't get angry. As a result, I developed the pattern of stuffing my anger down into my subconscious until it exploded in volcanic proportions.

I also entered marriage believing that as a godly Christian woman I should have no needs of my own but exist only to serve others. Looking back I realize Ted and I were a perfect match—a match that lit the flame of marital self-destruction. Ted was the risk taker with an addictive personality, and I was the ultimate codependent, ready to rescue at a moment's notice.

Fortunately, during our fifth year of marriage we attended a marriage enrichment weekend. The seminar hosts literally sequestered us in a hotel, took away our watches, and had us write letters to each other explaining our true feelings about issues that affected us both. We began with topics like finances, communication, raising children, dreams, and then the biggie: sex.

In addition to believing my own needs were unimportant, I had grown up in a family that avoided any discussion of sex. Those factors made my enjoyment of our lovemaking during those first five years of marriage hit-and-miss. We did it, but we never talked about it. In addition, my "pleaser" tendencies sometimes led me to fake an orgasm rather than hurt my husband.

The marriage enrichment weekend, however, brought me to a crossroads. I could choose either to be open with my feelings or continue the masquerade. I asked myself, *Will the sexual enjoyment I experience now work for the long haul?*

*If we remain married for another thirty years, will this level
of satisfaction be enough? Is this all there is?*

In spite of the risks, I chose to be open. I found it easier
than I thought to write out my questions and frustrations.
In the safe setting of the weekend conference, Ted met my
openness with his understanding, and the flame grew.

Obstacles to Intimacy

That day in the marriage conference, God brought me some
new and important insights. I realized that as Ted and I began
openly discussing our needs, we reached a new level of intimacy. I also realized that in one sense I was responsible
for my own orgasm. I needed to discover, explore, and take
responsibility for my sexual needs and then communicate
them clearly and appropriately to my husband. If I didn't
find satisfaction, no one could ultimately shoulder the blame
but me.

Of course, communication can take nonverbal as well as
verbal forms. Few husbands have the ability to read their
wife's mind. Since each woman has different needs and enjoys
pleasure in different ways, someone has to communicate. In
fact, areas of sexual need and desire often vary depending on
the woman's monthly cycle. When a husband realizes the same
action or experience that brought enjoyment last week may
not work at all this week, he will recognize the importance
of fresh, honest, ongoing communication.

God created marriage to enable his children to enjoy a passionate intimacy whose flame intensifies with the passing of
time. In his classic work *The Screwtape Letters*, C. S. Lewis
emphasizes that pleasures come only from above. Pastor and
author John Piper agrees: "This is an astonishing view of
pleasure. Hell has never been able to produce one! It can
only misuse the ones that God created—in 'times,' 'ways,'
and 'degrees' [all Lewis's terms] that God forbids."[2] Scripture

supports this line of thought: "You will show me the path of life; in Your presence is fullness of joy; at Your right hand are pleasures forevermore" (Ps. 16:11 NKJV), and "Every good gift and every perfect gift is from above, and comes down from the Father of lights, with whom there is no variation or shadow of turning" (James 1:17 NKJV).

Since we know God created sex for pleasure, why is it that only 29 percent of women report they regularly have an orgasm? What about the other 71 percent?[3] Over the years I've counseled many women, and this led me to understand I was not alone when it came to experiencing roadblocks to intimacy and sexual enjoyment. Let's explore the various dimensions of physical, emotional, and spiritual hurdles. Each can serve as tremendous obstacles to the genuine intimacy God created us to enjoy.

Physical Roadblocks

Most of us realize sex can be physically painful, especially if a woman is not fully aroused when intercourse takes place. God created both sexes with the ability to experience arousal. For example, the clitoris has nine thousand nerve endings, but none of those are required for the act of procreation any more than the taste buds in our mouth are required for the act of eating. This fact underlines the good news that God designed our taste buds and nerve endings for pure pleasure. Sexual passion and intimacy are part of his divine design. He wants us to be Sexy Christians.

In order to understand and appreciate God's wonderful creation, we need to know certain facts about our physiology. When a woman is sexually aroused, her vagina lubricates and the tissue engorges with blood, making the area more pliable. The average woman's vagina is only about four inches deep, but with arousal it expands to approximately six inches. The length of the average penis during erection? Six inches—and that's no coincidence. Without sufficient arousal, a tight, dry, four-inch pocket will create a great deal of pain, especially as the penis hits forcefully against the cervix.[4]

So in order to avoid pain, many women need to experience arousal and even orgasm prior to intercourse. God has designed the arousal process to help make the experience of intercourse supremely enjoyable. Our bodies change, especially as we pass through the season of childbearing and travel on through to menopause. A woman who takes time to become aware of what's happening in her body in each new season will find herself well prepared to enjoy her sexuality throughout her life.

During the months when I nursed our first child, I experienced a huge hormonal drop. Not only that, I was somewhat depressed. I felt my breasts were primarily for my child rather than my husband and became defensive. It was a difficult time for both Ted and me. Thankfully, before nursing our second child I anticipated the changes and educated myself appropriately. Both Ted and I enjoyed the overall experience much more than we had with our first.

Another big change in our sex life took place as I began menopause. For the first time in years, intercourse was painful. After I added lubricants, the pain was completely alleviated. Next I noticed my sexual desires were waning. I chose to be proactive and began a regime of natural hormones. My doctor told me my overall hormone levels were very low and my testosterone level was almost nonexistent. Because natural hormones are not an exact science, she said we might need to make some adjustments after a few months.

I asked how I would know if there was too much testosterone. She assured me, "You'll know." Sure enough, a few weeks into the new medication, I noticed Ted smiling a lot more. Then, a few months into the hormonal regime, he looked exhausted. I decided to back off a little on the testosterone.

Emotional Roadblocks

Past sexual trauma and abuse can serve as huge obstacles to intimacy because they interfere directly with God's desire for us to enjoy the sexual union. We have observed a direct correlation between the depth of abuse and the difficulty a couple has in achieving intimacy. When wounding has struck the core of our sexual identity, emotional healing must also reach to the core. I believe we Christians have an advantage in finding this kind of deep restoration. Ted discussed the process in the preceding chapter when he wrote about the need to confront our own inner issues so true healing and intimacy can occur.

Remember, Jesus understands the shame and pain of abuse, and this includes sexual abuse. In spite of artists' renderings of the scene, Jesus wore no loincloth as he hung naked on the cross. History tells us public nakedness in that culture held incredible shame. Philippians 2:6–8 says Christ could identify with every aspect of human suffering because he was fully man and fully God. Scripture also says Jesus came to set the captives free (Luke 4:18).

I've witnessed Christ's power to free multiple times as women, through prayer and counseling, have returned emotionally to the moment(s) of abuse and allowed Christ to enter their emotional pain. There are many Christian counselors who can help women face the trauma of the past and move toward healing. Usually, though, we want to run away or medicate our pain rather than face it so that true healing can occur.

When we take responsibility for our own sexual fulfillment, we also take responsibility to seek healing for anything that can obscure the intimacy God intends us to have. When a woman's husband agrees to play an active role in the healing process, God seems to move in especially powerful ways as he breaks multiple emotional roadblocks.

One woman I counseled carefully processed the pain, loss, anger, and betrayal of sexual abuse. After that the time came for her to learn to trust her husband. Because of various triggers and physical memories, he had to avoid approaching his wife sexually in particular ways. His sensitivity, coupled with allowing her to say "no" or "stop" whenever she felt uncomfortable, began the process of retraining her limbic system. Gradually, she trusted him because when she said no, he honored her wishes. This in turn gave her a new sense of power over her own body and the fears of the past. Over time the two enjoyed new and deeper levels of intimacy. Lack of trust is a huge roadblock to biblical intimacy, but *renewed trust between partners is a divinely designed fire-starter that kindles the flame of passion.*

> *Lack of trust is a huge roadblock to biblical intimacy, but renewed trust between partners is a divinely designed fire-starter that kindles the flame of passion.*

Spiritual Roadblocks

I like to show the participants in our Sexy Christians Seminars two pieces of paper: one blue, one pink. I glue the pieces together and, when the glue has set, pull them apart. Some of the pink paper sticks to the blue and some of the blue sticks to the pink. When the bond breaks, each piece suffers harm. Jesus speaks of the mystery of two becoming one flesh.

> Have you not read that He who made them at the beginning "made them male and female," and said, "For this reason a man shall leave his father and mother and be joined to his wife, and the two shall become one flesh"? So then, they are no longer two but one flesh. Therefore what God has joined together, let no man separate.
>
> Matthew 19:4–6 NKJV

In our sex-saturated society, many people—even Christ-followers—don't realize the full implications of sex outside of marriage. The damaged pink and blue sheets of paper provide a graphic illustration of what Jesus says about the power of the sexual union.

> Do you not know that he who unites himself to a prostitute is one with her in body? For it is said, "the two will become one flesh." But he who unites himself with the Lord is one with him in spirit. Flee from sexual immorality. All other sins a man commits are outside his body, but he who sins sexually sins against his own body.
>
> 1 Corinthians 6:16–18

Ted and I have seen this Scripture played out in the lives of the couples we have counseled through the years. Many who have experienced extra- or pre-marital sex struggle in their marriage—the union where they ought to experience the most freedom. This occurs because past sexual attachments have formed deep soul ties that profoundly affect the present. The enemy uses these links to the soul to prevent the individual from enjoying the passion of true marital intimacy.

I counseled one woman who faced this struggle in her relationship with her husband. When we prayed together about her past sexual attachments, she revealed she had once lived in a commune. She couldn't even name all of her previous sexual partners. In order to break the power of these spiritual soul ties, she needed God's cleansing and forgiveness. First she asked God to forgive her for sinning against these unnamed men. Next she asked him to forgive her for sinning against her own body (1 Cor. 6:18). Finally she asked him to forgive her for sinning against him.

As we broke the soul ties and renounced the power the enemy had gained in her life because of her immorality, God showed me a spiritual picture of what was happening. I saw painful hooks embedded in this woman's body that connected her by lines to a host of men. Suddenly a giant pair of scissors came from heaven and cut every line. That day she walked out of my office with a new sense of freedom. Finally she could belong fully to her husband. The truth had set her free.

God tells us in Scripture that there are spiritual implications when we choose to walk sexually in our own ways rather than his ways. I once counseled a woman who was very upset because her husband was pressuring her to do some things she didn't feel comfortable doing sexually. I asked her about his specific requests. When she told me, I realized no sin was involved in anything he asked. Instead, these ideas would simply challenge this woman to become a little more adventurous and to step out of her comfort zone. So why the struggle?

As huge tears poured down her cheeks, I realized the problem ran deeper than the sexual acts themselves. I probed more deeply and learned both she and her husband, who were Christians when they met, had wanted to remain pure before marriage. During the dating process he pressured her to give in to him sexually and violated her values along with the boundaries she had set. She succumbed to his pressure, and some of the joy of their wedding day was stolen. Fast-forward to our counseling time, where I realized it was not the act but her husband's approach—the same one he used before marriage—that triggered her tears and resistance.

I encouraged her to go home and share with her husband that she had discovered the source of her struggles. The wounds given during their dating relationship were blocking their present intimacy. I suggested they pray together and ask forgiveness for sinning against their own and their partner's bodies and against God. They asked God to give them a fresh start in their sexual relationship.

I hoped this fresh start based on truth and forgiveness would give them both freedom to respond in the present without reflecting their hurtful past. When I asked this hurting woman to be open with her husband, I knew he would respond in understanding because he loved both God and his wife. The bottom line: *the combination of openness and understanding made a great fire-starter, creating the potential for more intimacy and passion than they had ever experienced.*

The Roadblock of Betrayal

Betrayal is another obstacle to intimacy we see all too often in our counseling work. When a woman finds out her husband is continually viewing pornography or has had an affair, she shuts down emotionally and physically. Most women want to forgive their husbands, but trusting them again takes time. Some of them find writing out their anger helps. This was true for the woman who penned the following soon after she discovered her husband was addicted to pornography and masturbation.

> Dear God,
>   I am experiencing the heart-breaking re-
> ality of learning that my husband is sat-
> isfying himself in a mental and physical
> affair with fantasy—substituting pictures
> for the warmth of my body and love.
>   I struggle so hard to compete with an
> illusion to which I can't possibly com-
> pare, with an availability I can't dupli-
> cate, doing things I can't imagine. My
> helpless heart is being left out of his
> love life. The presence of the "other"
> woman has taken residence in his heart. I
> want to dwell there alone.
>   God, I so want to be the object of my
> husband's desire. My heart longs to see
> the hunger in his smile for my lips, the
> twinkle in his eye anticipating my touch.
> I cry out to feel sexy simply because he
> delights in me!

> Oh, Lord, cause my husband to see what
> you made me to be for him—a precious
> jewel—without blemish, holding all my de-
> sire and all of myself for him. Kindle his
> desire for your very best!
> It's me, Lord.[5]

Our church sponsors Betrayed Heart classes for women who have experienced some level of sexual betrayal. I tell the women in these classes it is normal to feel numb and angry toward their spouse. Their wedding vows have been violated and the numbness and anger will continue until they see their husband taking three steps to restore healthy sexuality and intimacy.

1. He must show his wife he is *sincere* about restoring their relationship.
2. He must have the *ability* to do whatever it takes to walk in healing. Usually that means he joins a Pure Desire group for men. There he is made accountable to other men who also struggle with sexual issues.
3. He must demonstrate *durability* (a willingness to continue making positive changes) in the new actions he takes. Over the next three to five years, the combination of positive changes and accountability to others can result in a restoration of his wife's trust.[6]

When we make a decision to face and deal with the roadblocks that keep us from intimacy, powerful things happen. The woman who wrote the letter to God decided to be open about her pain and frustration, and she gave the letter to her husband. After reading her heartfelt petition, her husband joined a Pure Desire group for men at our church. He became accountable to these men and worked on healing his own wounds. Over time their marriage grew in intimacy, and in the years since that horrific discovery, they've gone on to help other married couples.

God can use our openness and understanding as a foundation for his marital miracles if we allow him full access to our lives.

God can use our openness and understanding as a foundation for his marital miracles if we allow him full access to our lives. Tim and Jennifer understand this. They have an amazing testimony of his healing power in the face of multiple addictions and years of infidelity. This couple accepted Christ through the Pure Desire ministry at our church and worked through some of their problems step by painful step. But a day came when God brought them to new levels of hurt and healing. This is how they described it:

Tim: My commitment to getting healthy was strong. I was building a relationship with God I never had before. I was working hard and peeling back the layers of my addictions that brought me back to places in my past I didn't ever want to look at again but had to examine to understand.

We were carefully rebuilding our foundation. But I didn't realize I had built it on sand until one day the Holy Spirit started speaking to me. I ignored him at first, but the voice would not go away.

One Saturday morning after my Pure Desire group, I went home and told Jennifer about three affairs I had fifteen years before—one of which was with her best friend.

Jennifer: That morning was like a bad dream. I was feeling devastation emotionally, yet I couldn't feel. I had been lied to for fifteen years by both my husband and my best friend. I had an inner voice that for years suspected something might have happened, but the lies and deception by Tim and my friend made me think I was imagining things.

I know now that God had prepared me for this final disclosure. Without God . . . I could not have dealt with this emotionally. He gave me the strength to understand that Tim was disclosing this to me now to be completely free of his guilt and shame. If he held on to that, not only would he not be able to heal completely, but our marriage would never have survived.

That very evening we went to a service and heard a teaching from the book of Joshua on how the walls of Jericho fell down. It was just like our relationship. The foundation we thought we had begun to build was on quicksand and now had completely sunk away to nothing. Diane and Ted prayed for our marriage and stood us on the solid rock to begin to rebuild our foundation.

Tim: As difficult and devastating as that disclosure was, it was the best thing that could have happened to save our marriage. . . . Through the associations with East Hill Church, we began a support network that included accountability, developing friendships, and healing teachings. Today our marriage foundation is being constructed of the hardest compounds: concrete, granite, titanium—and Jennifer would say, diamonds. . . . As with the story of the rebuilding of Jerusalem related in the book of Nehemiah, we recognized the problem in our relationship, prayed about it, received support, and through that support started to rebuild our relationship as God intended—on solid ground.[7]

God can redeem our past if we are willing to do what it takes to face the pain, eliminate obstacles, and foster openness and understanding. Remember, God designed us for intimacy, so he'll make a way for us to reach it. He wants us to be Sexy Christians.

Love Lessons

We must take responsibility for our own sexual fulfillment.

As strange as it sounds, ultimately we are responsible for our own sexual fulfillment. No, God does not intend us to meet our own sexual needs. Instead, he intends to live his life, health, and wholeness through ours so this area—along with every other area of our lives—reflects his creative power.

As marriage partners, we have the responsibility of knowing our own sexual needs and then adequately and appropriately communicating them to our mate. We must also become aware of any areas of personal wounding that affect our relationship and seek healing, health, and restoration by following biblical models.

Openness and understanding act as fire-starters that ignite passion and true marital intimacy.

Scientific research as well as personal and professional experience prove a powerful connection exists between openness (transparency and vulnerability) and understanding (caring and acceptance). The more the two overlap in a couple's relationship, the more the partners will experience genuine intimacy. Great sex comes from a great heart: the heart of God, who designed us for intimacy, and the heart of two loving partners who allow God to change them from the inside out.

Physical, emotional, and spiritual roadblocks that serve as obstacles to marital intimacy often exist in the lives of one or both partners. Confrontation and confession must take place before these roadblocks can be removed. But consistent responses from the offending partner (including action and accountability) must also occur before trust is rebuilt and intimacy restored.

Home Play

Rules in review: (1) Avoid "you" statements. Instead, talk about your own actions, thoughts, and feelings. (2) Listen. Don't give advice or attempt to psychoanalyze your spouse. (3) If tempers flare, disengage and pray.

1. On a scale of 1–10 (1 low; 10 high), rate your level of satisfaction with the type and amount of affection you are giving and getting in your relationship with your spouse.

   <u>1   2   3   4   5   6   7   8   9   10</u>

2. On the same 1–10 scale, rate your level of satisfaction with the frequency and quality of sex in your relationship.

   <u>1   2   3   4   5   6   7   8   9   10</u>

3. How many times would you like to have sex each week?

   _____

4. Are you aware of any sexual problems in your lives? Write a few words here to describe them. When you and your spouse have both finished answering these questions, take time to pray together and discuss the results.

12

The Fiery Mountain of Intimacy

How Much Will True Intimacy Cost?

T E D

Our first camping experience: I remember it well, especially since it nearly ended our marriage. We had only been married a few months, and I talked my bride into a mountain-climbing trip. I felt sure we were in for a great adventure. My plan was that we would climb a 10,000-foot mountain together and spend the night at the summit. As we began our journey, I took off as though I was in a footrace and assumed Diane would be right there beside me. Instead, she was taking time to enjoy the view. She even asked me to carry her pack!

Before long the trail became precipitous and the oxygen molecules seemingly nonexistent. The farther we hiked, the more upset I became. *She's taking forever to catch up! And carrying two packs? I may as well have the mountain on my back!*

In the meantime, Diane had her own negative thoughts: *This new husband of mine is trying to kill me! Doesn't he ever stop to smell the roses?*

When we finally reached the summit and made camp, it was nearly dark. We were famished, so I pulled out the can of stew I had packed and placed it on the campfire. One problem: we had reached an altitude of over 10,000 feet, and I hadn't thought about how the change in altitude might affect our meal preparation. Incidentally, that phrase soon became my standard line for many aspects of our marriage: *I hadn't thought about that!*

At high altitude the boiling temperature of the stew was so low you could stick your finger in it and get frostbite. Finally, we decided the dog needed the stew more than we did. We dumped it into his bowl and went to bed exhausted.

In a fit of romantic stupidity, Diane and I had purchased a double sleeping bag. We ended up pulling against each other all night. During the constant tug of war, we also found ourselves sliding into the snowbank beside our tiny camp-site. And sometime in the middle of the long night our dog began to shiver so violently from the cold that his teeth were rattling.

That's when Diane made a fatal error. She invited the dog to crawl into the sleeping bag alongside us. He kept sticking his legs straight out, which allowed a hurricane force of arctic wind to blast into the sleeping bag every time. Just when I thought it couldn't get any worse, it did. In the middle of the night, the cheap stew cooked off in our dog's tummy with thermonuclear force. You've heard of weapons of mass destruction? Diane and I found ourselves gasping for air between moments of violent shivers as we raised our heads out of the now toxic sleeping bag and into the icy wind.

The morning hike down the mountain was a grim event. Diane wouldn't speak to me. She wouldn't even look at me.

I'm sure I saw some of the trees pulling back as she walked past, afraid they might ignite from the heat of her anger alone. And the dog? Well, he was walking kind of funny. I kept him behind me because the stew was still generating occasional moments of spontaneous combustion.

Little did I realize our marriage would experience many of its own moments of spontaneous combustion in the years ahead. And I certainly didn't understand that God would use those painful events to lead us to the fiery mountain of intimacy—exactly where we most needed to go.

To Know What We Can't Know Otherwise

Eventually I began to ask myself the question, *Why does God take us to the mountain?* The only answer that makes any sense is that he wants us to encounter the fiery heights of true intimacy with him and with each other.

Genesis 22 gives the account of when God called Abraham to the mountain. I remember the first time I read the disturbing words the Lord spoke to the aged patriarch.

> God tested Abraham's faith and obedience. "Abraham!" God called.
>
> "Yes," he replied. "Here I am."
>
> "Take your son, your only son—yes, Isaac, whom you love so much—and go to the land of Moriah. Sacrifice him there as a burnt offering on one of the mountains, which I will point out to you."
>
> Genesis 22:1–2 NLT

Those words became particularly unsettling to me when I realized that, according to the New Testament, if we've said yes to Christ we are also descendants of Abraham (Gal. 3:6–7). The words of Genesis 22 suddenly became more personal, and my question about why God calls us to the mountain became profoundly relevant.

Fortunately, the author of Hebrews answers this question. He says that God essentially told Abraham, "I want you to know what I'm going to do with my Son. The only way you can know how I feel is if you take your son and offer him as a sacrifice" (see Heb. 11:17–19). This also explains why, when Abraham raised the knife to slay Isaac, God declared through the mouth of an angel, "Don't lay a hand on that boy! Don't touch him! Now I know how fearlessly you fear God; you didn't hesitate to place your son, your dear son, on the altar for me" (Gen. 22:12 Message).

God takes you through some experiences just so you can *know*. In fact, you and your spouse can only know true intimacy by facing life's trials and triumphs together. I believe this is one of the reasons God chose the term *to know* as his primary way of describing sex. Paul, in his passionate prayer in Ephesians, cries out for us to know something we can't know otherwise: the love of Christ that surpasses mere knowledge (Eph. 3:19).

I remember the first time I looked through a night vision scope in combat (they weren't standard issue in those days). Suddenly I could see how the enemy could mask his movements and get so close to us before he attacked. Now I could understand his plan. *I came to know.*

In other words, some things require that you go through them in order to *know*. Without experience, you can *think* they are true, even *believe* they are true, but it's not until after you've gone through them that you can say, "I know whom I have believed and am persuaded that He is able to keep [this marriage] I have committed to Him until that Day" (2 Tim. 1:12 NKJV).

I have spent time with some brilliant scholars and found them intimidating. Great musicians can also be intimidating. (Of course, with my lack of musical skills, almost any musician is intimidating.) Since I love cosmology, I've listened to some scary smart astrophysicists, and they can be very intimidating too. But when it comes to knowing

God, I am not easily intimidated. I say this because I've been through some tough times in which God has exquisitely proven himself—and many of those painful times took place in my marriage.

When you come out on the other side, you *know*. You know God is at work in your marriage, and you know more about yourself than you care to know. It all balances out beautifully because in this process you come to know more about God than you ever thought possible. You realize he is not limited by your minuscule thought processes. His love is far deeper than you imagined; his grace is far wider than you hoped. You don't get that kind of knowledge out of a book or a lecture. Instead, you must go to the fiery mountain of intimacy with God when he calls you. He'll go with you to the mountain and pull something out that you never realized was there. *God calls us to the mountain so we can know what we can't know otherwise.*

Pain with a Purpose

Recently Diane and I counseled a young couple in which the husband was wrestling with an addictive mindset. He couldn't see it, which is normal, but he had a wife who loved him deeply and was encouraging him graciously. When I pointed out what a gift God had given him in her, I commented on the way Diane's love for me has called forth great things from my heart. On almost every occasion when this occurred, however, I was on a mountaintop dealing with God and my pain. In Abraham's culture, fathers found their value and future in their heritage—particularly in their firstborn sons. In this environment it seemed almost natural for Abraham to develop an unhealthy addiction to Isaac. But do you see what God did? He loved Abraham enough to bring him to the knifepoint of finding his value solely in his relationship with his heavenly Father.

Abraham's predicament perfectly portrays the pain that sooner or later we all have to face. The silly example of our mountain-climbing trip is a metaphor for other marital struggles. I viewed my wife as a source of pain on the trip up the mountain because she wasn't doing what I wanted her to do. I wanted to conquer the mountain and reach the top as quickly as possible. She wanted to enjoy the trip and spend time with me.

What we do with our pain is one of life's determining factors. Whether it's the pain of an inconvenience, a tragedy, or a trifle, it's what we do with it that counts. *What we do with our pain determines the depth of our character and the extent of our intimacy as a couple.* It also significantly affects the other members of the family, as we'll see before long.

Recent research underscores the importance of the way we deal with the pain that comes into our lives. This is illustrated below.

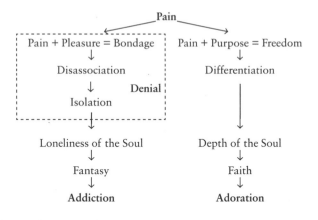

Interestingly enough, there are only two long-term options:

Option 1: Pain + Purpose = Freedom
Option 2: Pain + Pleasure = Bondage

The author of Hebrews helps us understand that Abraham believed God had a higher purpose in calling him to sacrifice his son. As a result, he came to know what he could not know otherwise. Abraham gained the freedom uniquely found in a true, deep, intimate knowledge of God.

Why does marriage bring so many struggles and so much pain? I believe this occurs primarily because we have been trained almost from birth to take option 2. For example, children usually develop the ability to perceive the emotion of shame during the second year of life. The same face-to-face interactions that stimulated excitement, exhilaration, and brain growth during the first year now include information on the recognition of disapproval and disappointment.[1] Of course this problem extends below the surface. Excessive shame lies at the root of nearly all addictive behaviors.[2] In fact, shame is such a powerful emotion that parents who overuse it can unwittingly predispose children to struggle with their emotions and their identity.[3]

What we do with our pain determines the depth of our character and the extent of our intimacy as a couple.

This dysfunction can continue indefinitely because research suggests that attachment patterns formed in childhood can last into adulthood. And attachment patterns have a significant effect on our experiences of romantic love, interpersonal relationships, and sense of self.[4] Translation: our past has programmed most of us to choose option 2 again and again.

This explains why God calls us to the mountain. In order to grow we must confront these deep attachment patterns. Since we have been wounded in relationship, God wants to heal us in relationship. But first we have to rid ourselves of the belief that our mate is the problem and quit saying to ourselves: *If my spouse would only change, my life wouldn't be so painful.* The Holy Spirit leads us to the mountain to change *us*, not our spouse.

Recently I was cruising YouTube and ran into a video clip of Sarah McLachlan singing her hit song "Angel." I was mesmerized. Her words perfectly encapsulated the book of Hosea in the Old Testament.

Hosea faced a painful, unusual challenge. God essentially told the prophet, "I want you to know something. I want to teach you about my love and grace. I want you to marry a hooker." Now that wouldn't have been a problem for a pimp. But for a prophet, especially one known for his message on holiness, that's another story entirely. I'm sure Gomer, the wife God chose for Hosea, was nowhere close to the person the young man had in mind when he thought of getting married. He had kept himself pure. "Hosea, I want you to feel what I feel," God said to him. "I want your life to illustrate what I'm going through because of my love for Israel," (see Hosea 1:2–3). The message is the same one Abraham received: "I want you to know what you cannot know, and the pathway is pain. There is a purpose for your pain." In other words, God was calling him to the mountain of divine perspective. Sarah McLachlan's words aptly reflect the heart of Hosea's bride: "You are pulled from the wreckage of your silent reverie."[5]

Gomer's life followed the pattern of repeating the same destructive behavior until Hosea (whose name means "salvation") came along and pulled her from the wreckage. The theme song of Gomer's life could be summed up by another phrase from McLachlan's song: "It is easier to believe in this sweet madness, Oh this glorious sadness that brings me to my knees."[6]

In my doctoral studies I had researched the book of Hosea extensively. I had translated, analyzed, and scrutinized it. But I had never read the book from Gomer's perspective. I had never read it with my heart.

Gomer's name means "complete" or "finished," but she is far from either one. God calls her to ascend to the mountain of true intimacy so she can learn her true identity. She has become accustomed to dealing with men, not love. She is skilled at having sex, not experiencing intimacy. But something in her soul says yes to Hosea's offer. And something within the heart of every human being cries out for true intimacy.

Journey to Intimacy

Why do so few couples experience deep, soul-satisfying intimacy? Why is it that so few Christian couples are truly Sexy Christians? The answer lies on the mountain.

Following God's call to the mountain of intimacy is never an easy journey. Ask Isaiah, who stood before the throne of God, crying out, "Woe is me!" Ask Daniel, who collapsed in the presence of the Ancient of Days as he saw the sweep of human history from beginning to end. Ask Abraham, who raised the knife over his own son. Ask Hosea, who watched Gomer sneak out the back door—again.

The journey of intimacy is as difficult for us as it was for Gomer. God called her into the present, but she struggled with her past. She tried hard to become a housewife. She put the evening meal on the table; she cleaned the house. God surrounded her with blessing, but she seemed unable to receive it.

Remember openness and understanding—the two fire-starters of true intimacy? We struggle to make them part of our marriages because of the shame and wounds we carry from our past. Let me speak clearly here: Perhaps you're frustrated because you are unable to receive the full blessing God wants to release in your life and your relationships. He clearly wants to take you to another level, and you sense that fact. But you can't get there until *you become comfortable with the person God says you are.*

Until you do, whenever you're under pressure you will almost always choose option 2 (Pain + Pleasure = Bondage). Most folks I counsel face the same mountain as Gomer; they struggle to receive God's blessing. But God calls us to his mountain of intimacy so we can know something we have no other way to know: *God loves us outrageously*. And whenever he wants to give us his blessing, the enemy brings up our past. That's why Gomer constantly struggled to see herself as Hosea did (Hosea 3:1–2).

God calls us to his mountain of intimacy so we can know something we have no other way to know: God loves us outrageously.

Do you understand that God sees you as holy, unblemished, the apple of his eye? You're the greatest part of his creation—greater than the galaxies, pulsars, or quasars. You name it; you top the list (see Gen. 1:31; Deut. 32:10; Rom. 8:19). Our struggles occur because we frequently allow the person we used to be to define the way we perceive ourselves today. This deadly cycle sets us up to deal with the pain in our life by seeking *pleasure* rather than trusting that God has a *purpose*. Whenever we choose option 2, we make crazy choices and find ourselves running from the intimacy we crave.

Every day Hosea went off to do whatever it is prophets do, and Gomer sneaked out the back door. Why? She was returning to the place from which she came in an attempt to gain comfort. When do we find ourselves seeking out the familiar? Not when things are going well but when we face pressure. That's when we return to what once comforted us. We go back to what we know, whether it's food, overwork, sex, booze, or compulsive spending. These comfort items help us medicate our pain.

God takes an entirely different approach. He wants to use our pain to take us to a level we cannot know. He wants us to move out of the place of pain to grasp the beauty of his activity in our life and our marriage.

Gomer was two different women in one body—a housewife and a hooker. She walked in the present but lived in the past. The amazing part of Gomer's story is that Hosea continued to love her. The amazing part of our story is that God continues to love us. Hosea kept loving Gomer even when she was sneaking out the back door. God keeps loving us even when our mind is sneaking out the back door. That all happens because of the finished work of Jesus Christ, not our efforts. That all happens because of the power of the shed blood of Christ, not our self-help programs. That all happens because of the dynamic power of the Holy Spirit's work in our life, not some positive thoughts we dream up. I am the person God says I am. I can do what God says I can do. And I can receive what God says I can have. Period.

Psychologists call this kind of deep self-understanding *differentiation*. I know who I am in Christ. I have been through enough tough times and chosen option 1 (Pain + Purpose = Freedom) so frequently that I know that I know who I am. I have learned to nurture myself in Christ regardless of how my mate may respond on any given day. Even the fact that my spouse may not be responding in the best way right now does not control my value and my emotions. Because of my deep relationship with Christ, I've developed the ability to face the pain intimacy brings.

Stuck in the Foothills

In our travels around the country and the world, I've often been surprised by how few Christian couples have a deep sense of intimacy in their relationship. As we discussed in chapter 1, most couples think intimacy is "being close and comfortable." This misconception sets you up to choose option 2 as a couple and leave the relationship stuck in the foothills of a stalemate.

Mark this: true biblical intimacy is developing the ability to get *uncomfortably close and vulnerable*. When your marriage is in stalemate mode, you find yourself caught up in crazy arguments about what really happened. Have you ever listened to a couple tell a story about their past only to end up in an argument over whose version is correct? Of course you have. You've probably done the same thing with your spouse. The real argument is about whose reality will become the dominant reality, whose anxieties will come out on top.

I call this the foothills of a stalemate because every couple has to pass through this area of their relationship on the way to the fiery mountain of intimacy. You see, climbing to the heights of intimacy requires faith, courage, and determination. You'll also need these to pass through some other foothills familiar to couples climbing toward intimacy—the *foothills of frustration*. That's the Sexy Christians term for the painful frustration that occurs when your mate fails to affirm you. Of course, mutual affirmation between spouses is vital to any relationship, but there are also times when one partner doesn't want to, cannot, or does not know how to affirm the other. Those painful moments help explain the *uncomfortably close* part of our definition of biblical intimacy.

If you intend to reach the fiery mountain of intimacy, you have to leave the foothills. Otherwise, your frustration over the pain can throw you into a quagmire of conflicting thoughts and accusations, which leads to a pit full of unforgiveness and personal reactions. As reality's boulders threaten to crush the deepest hopes of your heart, only the grace of God can carry you to the fiery mountaintop. Only the mercy of God can provoke you to confront your own wrong attitudes. And only the goodness of God can enable you to nurture yourself in Christ at the same time.

Partners who refuse to confront themselves begin confronting their spouse instead. In order to avoid the challenge of climbing to the high country of serving their mate in love, they instinctively try to control themselves, their partner, and the situation itself.

As we climbed the mountain together that day, the more slowly Diane went, the more controlling I became. I would much rather have climbed the physical mountain that lay before us than make myself face the greater challenge of my self-centeredness. I didn't want to pay the price of the climb toward true intimacy. And I certainly didn't want to grow up and recognize that not everything revolved around me after all. I wanted to stay in the comfortable—but crippling— corner of my little world.

Paying the Price

Like Gomer, some of us carry brokenness within. That day on the mountain I wasn't trying to be selfish; I didn't even realize what I was doing. I was simply reacting out of the deep mental patterns etched by my wounds from the past. And that's why Hosea's response to Gomer's sin still brings tears to my eyes. He heads into town asking everyone, "Have you seen my wife? She's been gone for three days. Have you seen her?"

> Her eyes used to light up when she came into a room and saw me.
> His heart used to open up when he came to our time of morning prayer.

> Have you seen her?
> Have you seen him?

Hosea goes down to the supermarket, still trying to find his wife. Next he heads over to the mall. She's not there either. The only place left to look is the slave market.

> The only place left to look for him is the porn shop.
> The next place to look is where long ago she bought drugs.

He would never return to that pit.

She would never go back to that pain.

But if you compromise long enough, if you make the easy option-2 choice rather than taking the narrow path of option 1, you'll find yourself in a place that's missing the touch of God. You'll be bought into slavery to something you once considered play.

Finally, Hosea finds Gomer on the sale block at the slave market. *Could that be her, with all those chains around her soul? Could that be her, with anger and sin, pride and jealousy crushing the life out her? Could that be her?*

Could that be the couple I blessed as they walked down the aisle together?

Could that be the same couple who now look more like ships passing in the night?

Could that be the same couple, living separate lives in the same house, caught up in their own hurts and fears rather than facing the battle together?

Could that be the same couple I called to the high country of passionate intimacy?

Could that be the same couple, now trapped in the bitter jail cells of their little lives?

I absolutely love the next part of the story. The Bible tells us Hosea doesn't walk away, withdraw, or say something his friends might want to hear like, "It's not worth it; she's gone too far. She doesn't understand me. She has so many wounds and hurts she's impossible to deal with."

Instead, the wronged husband does an amazing thing. He chooses to get uncomfortably close. He stops Gomer abruptly and says, "Wait a minute, I can't let the enemy take you. I can't let our relationship be destroyed. *I love you.* I know you don't believe anyone could love you, but I do. *I love you.*

I know you've done some wrong things. Yes, I know you've fooled around, but that doesn't change the fact that *I love you*. You don't understand how much. Please don't let them take you away. *I love you*. I'll pay the price."

In spite of its beauty, we can unconsciously relegate the story of Hosea and Gomer to the realm of myth or religious fairy tale unless we recognize its deep truth. This story is as current as today's headlines, as relevant as the most recent fight you had as a couple. It's a graphic picture of what Christ has done for each of us.

Each of us. I know; you may have been raised in the perfect Christian home as the perfect Christian child—the one who never did anything wrong. But no matter how good we may consider ourselves to be, we know our hearts are tainted and corrupt in contrast to God's pure holiness.

Christ didn't leave us on hell's auction block. He paid the price. None of us deserves it, but he paid for us with his own blood.

Because of his sacrifice, none of us has to live in the lowlands of a mediocre marriage. None of us has to settle for mere side-by-side existence, stuck in the foothills of a stalemate or frustration. We can live on the fiery mountain of intimacy. We can get uncomfortably close and vulnerable. We can open up and share truthfully even at the risk of deep pain. Yes, we'll face fire and pain, but we're willing to pay the price because we've caught a glimpse of the mountaintop and the wonders it holds.

The depth of our relationship with our spouse relates directly to the depth of our relationship with God. In our moments of deepest hurt and frustration, we can turn to him for comfort and nurture. In the process, an amazing paradox takes place. We come to know what we cannot know otherwise about ourselves and about our God. We step past the offense and fall more deeply in love with each other. We climb to the mountains of deep intimacy and incredible passion. Finally, we recognize this is nothing less than an incredible

gift from our heavenly Father—a Father who loves us enough
to pay the price.

Love Lessons

*God calls us further into intimacy so we can know what we
can't know otherwise.*

God's purposes in intimacy run deep. Since he created
us for relationship, we learn, grow, hurt, and heal within
the context of our interactions with others and with God
himself.

God longs for us to know him more—and to know our spouse
more—so he calls us to the mountain
of intimacy alongside him. We come
there to know what we can't know
any other way. When we spend time
with him, we know. When he sustains
us through painful circumstances, we
know. When he enables us to love during a season when our spouse can't
or won't meet our needs, we know.
In truth, we can't know (gain deep
knowledge) in our own strength or
power. We can only know through
the relationships of the fiery mountain of intimacy.

*The depth of our
relationship with our
spouse relates directly
to the depth of our
relationship with God.*

*What we do with our pain determines the extent of our
intimacy as a couple.*

No matter what kind of pain we have, it's what we do with
it that counts. We all experience pain. We all have a choice
about how we respond. We can deny and withdraw or self-
medicate (Pain + Pleasure = Bondage), or we can choose the
high road of self-confrontation that leads us into healing.

We can also choose to acknowledge God and his purposes
in the midst of our pain. When we bring him our hurts and
failures, he listens and restores. When we bring him our prob-

lems, he makes a way for us to endure. When we see God in the midst of our pain, our hearts change. We stop blaming others. We take responsibility for our actions—good and bad. And we grow in intimacy with our spouse and with God. Pain + Purpose = Freedom!

Home Play

Rules in review: (1) Avoid "you" statements. Instead, talk about your own actions, thoughts, and feelings. (2) Listen. Don't give advice or attempt to psychoanalyze your spouse. (3) If tempers flare, disengage and pray.

1. Do you have a funny story about a time that could have drawn you into intimacy but ended as spontaneous combustion instead? Draw a simple cartoon about this time. Show it to your spouse and discuss the memories it evokes.

2. Nearly everyone knows a marriage where a "Hosea" (male or female) has paid a tremendous price to forgive and redeem a "Gomer" (male or female). Write down the initials of a couple who could fit this category. If appropriate, discuss it with your mate.

3. Think about a time in your marriage or your life that caused you great pain but taught you to know what you could not know otherwise. Describe it below in as few words as possible and discuss it with your spouse.

4. Have you been a person who routinely chooses option 2 (Pain + Pleasure = Bondage)? Think back to your childhood and a time when you used pleasure to medicate your pain. Describe the experience of making that choice. Use a single word to describe the results. Use another word to describe the emotions you felt afterward. If possible, take time to share the memory with your partner.

Part 4

Biblical Intimacy

God Reflects His Image through Biblical
Intimacy—the Uncomfortably Close
Relationship between a Husband and Wife

13

The Wonder of It All

What's So Great about This Intimacy Stuff Anyway?

TED

My astronomy class tumbled out behind me as I stepped out of the van. The young men and women quickly ran toward the observatory, their breath visible in the cold night air. They laughed and jostled one another along the way. The gravel crunched beneath our feet with the distinctive sound that comes on a cold, clear night. As I looked upward from Manastash Ridge, it seemed as though I could see forever. The night itself seemed to fall silent—a reverent response to the magnificent display of God's glory.

I was teaching an astronomy course for a local Bible college. That might seem like another oxymoron, but I had somehow talked the administration into offering the course. In my view, science and faith should be allies, never enemies. The class became immensely popular with the students. Few were great scientists, but nearly all were great lovers of knowledge.

This love became apparent as we crowded around the thirty-inch Cassegrain telescope. The observatory had no scientific observations scheduled for the evening, so we had the telescope at our disposal. The director asked what we would like to see first. Immediately I responded, "The Crab Nebula!" As the telescope slowly tracked across the evening sky to focus on that distant star, I reminded the class what we had learned about this supernova.

In the summer of 1054 Chinese astronomers reported a star that suddenly became as bright as the full moon. We now understand that a spectacular supernova explosion took place. The remains of this detonation of a massive star are now visible as the Crab Nebula. Although the core collapsed, it still exists in the form of a rotating neutron star. The students and I had the incredible opportunity to observe one of the most fascinating astronomical objects known to modern science.

It is one thing to see a picture of the Crab Nebula in astronomy textbooks; it's entirely another thing to see it with your own eyes. One by one the students looked through the telescope. I could see the sense of awe in their faces. There on the observation deck we celebrated a spontaneous worship service. The students huddled together in the cold as we raised our hearts and hands in praise.

Image of God

By now you understand that *God has called us to be more than just people who have sex; he has called us to be Sexy Christians.* You also understand by now that a Christian's sexuality holds incredible meaning. You recognize it from the first chapters of the Bible where you first hear God's creative cry. That heart cry was not, "Let us create pulsars, galaxies, and the cosmos." God did it all in preparation for his most creative moment, the moment that represents the ultimate expression of earthly beauty: the creation of humanity. "So God created man in his own image, in the image of God he created him; male and female he created them" (Gen. 1:27). That one verse reveals as nowhere else in the Bible the nature of the spiritual purpose, power, and passion God has enfolded into our sexuality. It also reveals why this area can create such colossal conflict.

God has called us to be more than just people who have sex; he has called us to be Sexy Christians.

Your gender is a fundamental aspect of your life. Our sexuality is also a foundational flashpoint in our battle with the forces of hell. Why? There are only two places on this planet where the world has a chance to see the image of God: (1) in the healthy relationships between men and women in the church (Eph. 5:30–32), and (2) in a covenant relationship between husband and wife.

The image of God is not visible in the snowcapped majesty of Mount Hood in my backyard or in the wild and rugged beauty of the Oregon coast nearby. Neither is it seen in any areas of natural beauty located close to your home. These arenas of geographic splendor are samples of God's handiwork—only samples. But when a husband and wife come together physically, emotionally, and spiritually, Scripture records the following amazing fact: *the image of God is revealed.*

I often tell couples, "The holiest room in your house is the bedroom." Of course I use those words deliberately. But what a startling statement that is to some individuals—especially those raised with a negative or "dirty" view of sex.

Next I say, "Your spiritual adversary absolutely hates the image of God. He understands God has one soft spot: his love for you. The enemy will attack you in an attempt to wound the heart of God. He especially wants to attack your sexual unity and intimacy as husband and wife. If his attack succeeds, he can accomplish two things at once: (1) he can strike the heart of God, and (2) he can deface God's image on this planet."

Because of the enemy's attacks, people in our world have an increasingly distorted view of God. If Satan can bring sexual bondage into your relationship and your life, he gains a huge victory. Your witness becomes a joke. You may look great on the outside, but your spiritual impact will be feeble at best.

Legacy

The phone call broke my heart. He was a nationally known religious figure—you would recognize his name if I mentioned it. But he was deeply entangled in sexual bondage. A friend had recommended that he call me. As I listened to his comments, two things stood out: First, he was a phenomenal communicator. If he had taken up an offering, I likely would have given him all I had. Second, the depth of his addiction broke my heart. I asked a few questions about his background, and the location of his pain quickly became obvious.

I knew he was medicating the pain through his sexual addiction. But when I suggested the possibility that the wounds of his past lay at the core of the darkness, he didn't get it. He blew it off and hung up with no promise to seek counsel in the areas of woundedness we had discussed.

Today this man's ministry footprints have been totally washed away—his name only remembered by the fall that made the evening news. On the outside it appeared as though he had a fruitful ministry. But behind the scenes, the enemy was tearing away at his soul.

Through the years I've discovered this man is far from alone. I recently wrote several articles for Rick Warren's *Min-*

istry Toolbox, a weekly online newsletter. Since Rick Warren has a huge following, the subscribers to this newsletter form an excellent cross-section of pastors across America. My final article contained a clinical tool designed to evaluate sexual addiction.

The results stunned even me. Over 50 percent of the pastors who took the evaluation fit the clinical definition of sexual addicts. And 24 percent of the women who took the evaluation could be considered addicts as well.[1] The church in America has experienced astonishing wealth and technical sophistication; no wonder there has been little—if any—change in our moral culture. Unless the church deals with this issue, we have no chance for a true revival that will change the moral climate of our nation. That is primarily why Diane and I have taken on the challenge of writing this controversial book.

Parents, beware. If you don't contend for sexual health in your own lives, you can pass an addictive mindset to the next generation. God makes it clear: addictive behavior moves from one generation to the next (Exod. 20:5–6). Clinical studies verify this fact.[2] Today's young people are becoming unusually vulnerable to sexual addiction. In fact, the primary users of internet porn are now twelve- to seventeen-year-olds.[3] Healthy sexual passion between a husband and wife in today's world goes beyond mere pleasure to the divinely ordained purpose of leaving a powerful spiritual legacy in a hopeless, helpless world.

What Is Normal?

In this final chapter I want to underline the fact that biblical intimacy goes far beyond a changing jolt of passion; it encompasses an entire journey. This means some critical conversations must occur along the way.

In previous chapters we have repeatedly pointed to the radical differences between men and women. Will Rogers said, "There's two theories to arguing with a woman. Neither one works." As husband and wife you are never going to agree on everything. However, we must settle on some basics for this journey. The first is the issue of sexual frequency or *desire discrepancy*. When you're young and first become romantically involved, your anticipation of being together overrules any differences in hormone levels. But soon the novelty wears off and the differences in sexual drives surface.

Studies estimate 90 percent of couples experience tension in this area of their relationship *but never talk about it*. The individual with the lower sex drive essentially controls what happens. This can start a quiet war because we typically equate our sense of adequacy with the level of our spouse's desire for us. Since Satan loves to tweak any sense of inadequacy or low self-esteem, it's important to discuss any discrepancy in your levels of sexual desire. It will surface at some point. Of course you can't really talk about the issues until you make the choice to separate your sense of adequacy from your mate's level of sexual desire for you. Discuss the issue and begin to free yourselves from the enemy's bondage.

In terms of sexual frequency, the issue of what is *normal* always comes up, especially among men. I remember one speaker at a men's gathering trying to communicate the truth that when it comes to sexual frequency, *normal* does not exist. The definition depends on the couple.

The speaker decided to illustrate his point, so he started asking the men to raise their hands in response to his questions. "Men," he asked, "how many of you have sex with your wife numerous times per week?" A number raised their hands, especially the macho types.

Then he asked, "How many of you have sex with your wife once a week?" A larger number of men raised their hands. The speaker noticed a man in the back of the room who was smiling from ear to ear.

Next he asked, "How many you have sex with your wife twice a month?" A few more men raised their hands.

"How many of you have sex with your wife once a month?" he asked. The guy in the back of the room still sat with a smile from ear to ear, but he hadn't raised his hand.

The speaker asked, "How many have sex once every two months? Once every six months?"

The man still hadn't raised his hand. Finally the speaker asked, "How many have sex just once a year?" The guy's hand shot up and his smile grew even broader.

"Sir," the speaker asked, "is it true you only have sex with your wife once a year?"

"That's right," the man fired back.

"Then may I ask why you're smiling from ear to ear?"

The guy beamed even more broadly and declared for everyone to hear, "*Tonight's the night!*"

I don't know whether this story is true, but it illustrates my point: when it comes to sexual frequency, there is no *normal*. You and your mate need to address this subject as a couple.

One of the major reasons we can exhibit such low sexual desire in marriage is we're often too pooped to party. The pace of life in our world today can only be classified as insane. I think one of the real enemies of a fulfilling marriage is fatigue. And yet the most important commitment you will ever make in your life outside of your commitment to God is the commitment you've made to your spouse. That's also why the New Testament tells us the only time we can set aside the sexual aspect of our marriage is for a mutually agreed-upon time of prayer (1 Cor. 7:4–6).

When you're tired all the time, intimacy doesn't happen. That's why you should take at least one night a week as your night out together. If you're too broke to pay for a babysitter, find another couple who is equally broke and trade kids so you can each have a date night.

Healing Grace

This brings us to another critical conversation you need to have along the way. When the kids first show up, you suddenly find yourself in desperate need of two things: sleep and sanity. The arrival of children will definitely destroy any previous order your life had. And once your wife begins to nurse a baby, her prolactin levels go through the roof and her sexual desire falls through the floor.[4] High prolactin levels lead to decreased sexual desire and arousal as well as difficulty in lubrication. Abstinence is not only for singles; it goes along with being married and having children.

So many times I have heard a young man say to me in the counseling office, "I thought marriage would cure my struggle with masturbation."

"Marriage doesn't cure your sexual problems; it only makes them more deadly if they're not confronted and dealt with," I respond. I constantly tell single men, "Get healthy sexually as a single. Don't drag this stuff into a marriage. Get into a Pure Desire group for men *now*."[5]

Nearly every week a married man walks into my office with *that look* on his face. By now I've learned to check his backside. Sure enough, he sports the footprint of a woman's shoe smack in the middle of his hindquarters. His wife has demanded he come see me. So I ask right up front, "Do you really want to meet with me?"

Usually his answer is vague. "Well, kind of. My wife caught me looking at porn. I don't think it's that big of a deal."

I lay my cards on the table. "Sir, if you don't want to be here, let's not waste your time and mine. Real intimacy is not for the uncommitted. If you want to have a fantastic sex life and experience deep intimacy with your wife, two things need to happen. First, you have to confront yourself. Second, out of this self-confrontation, you must self-disclose with your partner."

That's never a popular statement, so I say, "Okay, you put your check in the box. You saw me. Let's call it a day. But when the pain level gets high enough, you come and see me again." This gentleman has no idea what kind of battle he faces.

He also doesn't have a clue that this is all a giant setup from God. He doesn't realize he's been using his sexual behavior to medicate his wounds from the past. God wants to deal with that problem by means of his marriage.

Some psychologists say that at a subconscious level we choose our mate out of a need to complete our unfinished childhood business. We have effectively freeze-dried our imperfect parents in our childhood memories, and we reconstitute them in our partner.[6]

Thankfully, the clinical evidence to support such a statement is rather thin. I believe a much deeper truth is at work in the selection of our mates. After counseling couples for nearly thirty years, I'm convinced that God's sovereign hand intervenes for those who invite Christ into the process. *Our loving heavenly Father handpicks our mates to participate in our healing.* He uses them uniquely to heal the wounds of our past and strengthen our lives today.

Oftentimes, I have found myself reacting to Diane, only to realize I was actually reacting to my mother. At times Mom's alcoholism triggered her to smother me with over-the-top concern. Well, my wife is a natural problem solver. She loves to ask all kinds of questions about how I intend to fix something. If I'm not careful, her inquiries can remind me of the way Mom used to pelt me with questions. Diane's questions, however, come from a completely different motive. I had to confront my past wounds before I could recognize the present truth: my wife's tendency to prod me with questions is all a sovereign setup by a loving and gracious God.

Opposites tend to marry one another. We're drawn to strengths we don't possess. But in marriage, past attractions quickly become present frustrations. We see the orderliness as obsessive-compulsive or the adventurous spirit as pure recklessness. This disconnect lies at the core of most marital arguments about whose reality is correct. In order to grow in an area of life that isn't our natural strength, we must move out of our comfort zones and see life from a new perspective. Marriage, as no other relationship, brings us into challenging confrontations with fresh realities.

We must understand that our struggles don't all disappear when we come to Christ. They don't all end on our wedding day either. In fact, it seems as though the struggles increase because we're suddenly confronted at close range by issues we never knew existed. In some mysterious way, however, on the day we marry we also meet our healer, our patient, and our fellow struggler. We meet the one person Christ will uniquely use to bring his transforming power to bear on our lives.

On the day we marry we also meet our healer, our patient, and our fellow struggler. We meet the one person Christ will uniquely use to bring his transforming power to bear on our lives.

Intimacy is an incredibly challenging journey. We go from the rapture of the honeymoon period, to the crucifying impact of deep confrontations with our selfishness, to the frustrating foothills of a stalemate. Each part of the process demonstrates the loving hand of a gracious God. He brings healing deep into our lives so we can ascend the fiery mountains of intimacy together.

Intimacy happens when the *purpose* of your life together goes so far beyond anything you could have experienced on your own that it astounds you. Intimacy happens when you look into your spouse's eyes and lose yourself in the *power* of God's mercy, love, and forgiveness. Intimacy happens when your *passion* transcends words and touches you so profoundly it moves you to the depths of your soul. Now that is biblical intimacy. And that is life as a Sexy Christian.

Honest to God

Unfortunately for many couples, these words seem like nothing more than romantic metaphors. Yet intimacy is God's ultimate purpose for our relationship with him and with our mate. That's why I want to encourage you to pick up the companion to this book, the *Sexy Christians Workbook*. We've filled it with page after page of exercises to help guide you as a couple through the journey of biblical intimacy. It is an expanded version of the Home Plays you have read here, with built-in time for additional interaction, discussion, and fun.

Diane and I tell couples who participate in our Sexy Christians Seminars that the exercises we ask them to do are worth at least $2,000 of counseling. In the evaluations following Sexy Christians Seminars, the most frequent comments we receive reflect their time of sharing with each other:

> "We have never talked about this stuff in twenty years of marriage."
> "It lit a new depth of passion between us."
> "I was amazed it brought healing into areas of our relationship that have been dysfunctional for years."

Those comments came from only one forty-five minute session of couples talking with one another. Just think what could happen in your marriage if you walked through the entire workbook together. Things at home could really heat up.

I know better than most people how challenging this area can be. The only other option, however, is death on the installment plan. I have seen so many couples who commit to making progress move into a level of health and intimacy in their marriage they never dreamed was possible. These folks had the most critical conversation of all: they came before God and before each other with total honesty.

Why do we find it so hard to have an honest conversation with God? The answer to this question is critical because the depth of intimacy we have with our partner directly reflects our intimacy with God.

The conclusion I've reached may shock you; it certainly surprised me. I've discovered God believes some outrageous things about me. It's funny, though; the only definition of myself that matters is the one God has for me. And guess what? God is scandalous in his love. He tells me things like:

I am holy and without blame before him in love (Eph. 1:4).

I have been sealed for him with the Holy Spirit. The blessings I experience now from him are just a foretaste of the great things he has planned ahead for me (Eph. 1:13–14).

I am called of God for a divine purpose (2 Tim. 1:9).

I don't know about you, but those kinds of truths are hard for me to accept. I grew up hearing, "You're a mistake." You see, I was an illegitimate child. *You don't have the right to experience joy and fulfillment. You're not allowed to make a mistake; you have to prove yourself.* When you grow up in the home of an alcoholic with abusive stepfathers, those thoughts are pounded deep into your soul. I can still hear one of my stepdads telling me, "You're no good, kid. You'll never be a real man." Most of us have a sinister voice like that somewhere deep inside.

But what does all this have to do with sexual fulfillment and intimacy? Let me put it this way: more than 80 percent of the men I've counseled who are struggling with deep sexual issues have a cavernous father wound. And research has uncovered the fact that being raised in a rigid, disengaged home makes people uniquely vulnerable to addictive behavior.[7]

Face the Facts

You may wonder, "Are you saying that being raised in a dysfunctional family dooms you to struggle the rest of your life?" My answer is a resounding, "No, of course not. Christ died to set you completely free!" But I need to add a very important qualifier: *You must be willing to face your own issues.* Remember, being forced to face your inner wounds is one of the character-building gifts marriage brings you.

The Holy Spirit will use some unexpected healing methods in your life to bring you to the point of honesty. One afternoon I was putting the finishing touches on my weekly sermon. This one dealt with God's love for each of us. It was a great teaching, and I was excited to share it with my flock. I knew God would use it to heal some deep inner wounds.

Suddenly, the Holy Spirit spoke to my heart: *You can't share that with the flock until you settle things with your father.*

I spoke back immediately, *Excuse me; I didn't even know the jackass!*

I call this principle *facing the facts of your freedom.* When you have a deep wound in your soul (and we all do), God brings it to your attention and challenges you to face the pain and trust in his love for you. Then you wipe your eyes and say, "Thank God, that's over."

But wait; there's more. Later in life you'll find yourself facing another painful issue in your life, crying again, and inviting the Holy Spirit to come and touch your heart at an even deeper level.

"And that's good news?" you may ask.

It really is. At the point of your deepest hurt, you'll discover your deepest hope. You'll also recognize the amazing nature of your calling in Christ. As Paul says, we become equipped to comfort others with the comfort with which God has touched our lives (2 Cor. 1:4). We discover the incredible paradox of the gospel: *where we are most weak is precisely where Christ makes us strong* (2 Cor. 12:9). That's another way the God of heaven and earth reveals his image in us.

The Wonder of It All

Not long ago as I was praying, I asked my heavenly Father, *Father God, I don't have a grandson from my son's side of the family. I have a grandson through my daughter, and I'm so thankful for him. Now I know it might just be a macho thing, but I would like to see the Roberts family line continue. You pulled me out of so much.*

At the point of your deepest hurt, you'll discover your deepest hope. You'll also recognize the amazing nature of your calling in Christ.

I didn't recall that prayer until months later when my son asked if he and his wife could come visit. Upon their arrival they gleefully announced we were going to be grandparents again. I asked when this marvelous event would occur, doing mental calculations of a date nine months down the road. They beamed and told us, "It'll happen next week!"

"How?" Diane and I both wanted to know.

"We're adopting a cocaine baby. The child had cocaine in its urine, not its bloodstream. It appears to be totally healthy." At that point, my son put his hand on my shoulder and asked, "Dad, guess what his name is?"

"It's a boy?"

"He sure is, Dad, and we're naming him Benjamin Theodore Roberts."

That's my name, and that's when they had to scrape me up off the floor. I fell apart. God had heard my cry. He had taken this little guy, pulled him out of the hell of his birth situation, and made him part of our family. I was stunned by my heavenly Father's goodness and by the wonder of it all—this living, breathing picture of God's love for baby Ben and for me.

My prayer for the continuation of my family line rose from a desire to see God take the pain of the world and transform it. It rose from the ashes of the pain that ruled my life before I realized a gracious God had set me apart for blessing. And the prayer matched God's desire for our family to be an ongoing expression of Christ's beauty.

Baby Ben represents a delightful part of God's answer. I remember the first time I held him in my arms and looked deep into his wide eyes. I saw a beauty there that far exceeds what I had seen that night up on Manastash Ridge. Even the most beautiful scene on earth cannot remotely compare to the greatness of God revealed in a human heart touched by his love.

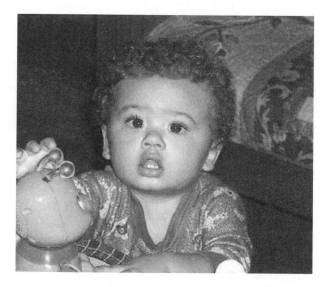

Every day Diane and I pray you will come to know how intensely God loves you. We pray you will learn to celebrate your sexuality as a reflection of the image of God. And finally, we pray you will truly become a Sexy Christian.

Love Lessons

Biblical intimacy is an expression of the image of God.

The heart of the Father is never more evident than through the glory of his creation; we see his wonders all around us. His image, however—the exact representation of his nature— is revealed only in two places: (1) the expression of his life in the church and (2) the total vulnerability and connection of a couple whose lives and hearts are surrendered to him (Eph. 5:30–32).

The enemy fights to gain control of our sexuality because he hates anything that so closely identifies us with the Father. Throughout our lives he whispers lies in his attempt to take us down through dysfunction, disengagement, and other weapons in his arsenal of destruction. Christ's redeeming work on the cross, however, means the final chapter has been written and the final victory won. When we choose openness and understanding, we also choose to step into the fullness of our life with him. That's the power, passion, and purpose of biblical intimacy and the surrendered life of a truly Sexy Christian.

Home Play

Rules in review: (1) Avoid "you" statements. Instead, talk about your own actions, thoughts, and feelings. (2) Listen. Don't give advice or attempt to psychoanalyze your spouse. (3) If tempers flare, disengage and pray.

1. The spoken word carries power, especially when it contains the truth of God's Word. Hold hands with your partner and look into one another's eyes. Speak the

following truths to each other, inserting your partner's name each time. (Feel free to add other truths as long as they come from Scripture.)

_____, you are holy and without blame before him in love (Eph. 1:4).

_____, you have been sealed for him with the Holy Spirit. The blessings you experience now are just a foretaste of the great things he has planned for your future (Eph. 1:13–14).

_____, you are called of God for a divine purpose (2 Tim. 1:9).

2. In this chapter, Ted describes marriage as "a giant setup from God." In other words, God specifically places us with a marriage partner whose strengths and weaknesses become part of our healing. Below, name two of your own strengths and weaknesses. Review these with your partner and discuss God's healing work in your lives.

3. Ted also refers to the fact that most couples never talk about their sexual frequency. Have you ever discussed this issue? How would you rate your level of lovemaking?

a. Poverty
b. Not nearly enough
c. Just about right
d. A bit of a challenge
e. Too much of a good thing

4. God gives every couple divine marital moments when they can see and sense his image through the glory of their union. Think back to such a time. Write one word below to help you remember it. Share your answer with your spouse. If possible, re-create the moment (or create a new one).

Appendix 1

Sexy Christians: Woman to Woman

DIANE

The red flags were waving long before our wedding, but I was young and sure our love could conquer anything. The problem: Ted's love for flying came before everything else. He warned me early on that if he ever had to choose between airplanes and me, the silver-winged creatures would win every time. I smiled, thinking I would soon change him and outmaneuver his lust for aluminum.

Marriage makes a great reality check—whether you want one or not. During our first two years of marriage, I spent many nights crying myself to sleep. Ted left every day at four in the morning and didn't return home until ten or eleven at night. He was determined to be one of the few Marines chosen to fly jets in a Navy training squadron. No sooner had he accomplished that goal than he was on his way to Vietnam. The huge transport plane took off down the runway for

South Asia, and the picture-perfect marriage I'd envisioned lay shattered in the dust.

Fast-forward twenty years. Our dusty white SUV meandered down the Canadian road that bordered the state of Washington while we looked for the turnoff to Raft Ranch. Ted was driving, so I concentrated on reading the directions aloud from the brochure he'd found. From the seats behind us, our two teenagers eagerly scanned the landscape, anticipating our first family raft trip down the whitewater rapids of the Chilliwack River. The brochure promised a beautiful family campground, a hearty barbeque meal, and (my favorite part) a relaxing soak in a hot tub after our rafting adventure.

I looked at the joyful faces of the people on the brochure as they hit a Class 4 rapid, then closed my eyes and tried to envision Raft Ranch. I assumed it might be a little rustic, so my mind clicked through the western television programs I had seen as a child. My thoughts pictured our destination as a cross between the Big Valley and Ponderosa Ranch. I smiled.

Reality Check

The directions led to a dirt road and down to the river. When we reached the bottom of the hill I knew we had taken a wrong turn. The only visible building, a lean-to garage, looked like Laura Ingalls Wilder's first little house on the prairie. Disappointment filled my heart as I realized this was, in fact, Raft Ranch. The family campground was an open, overgrown field with no running water or electricity. The barbeque area was a cement slab with an open metal roof hung over the picnic tables, and the hot tub was a large barrel the ranch staff boasted would hold ten people. As they struggled to fill it with tap water, they assured me after a chilly five-hour ride down the river, it would feel like a hot tub.

Maybe we can get our money back, I thought. *After all, it's raining off and on.* Word came down from the owner: no refunds. At that point I decided to hide my disappointment. After all, our kids were focused on the river trip ahead and seemed unfazed by the dilapidated surroundings. I could do this—for their sake.

We headed to the restrooms before putting on our wet-suits. When we turned the corner, we saw three outhouses awaiting our arrival. *Little House on the Prairie* again! My disappointment changed to laughter as I opened the door of the first small building. I had to look at the other two to make sure. Sure enough, each had its own basket of beautiful fresh flowers attached to the inside wall.

Most of us have Big Valley visions of what marriage will be like. Soon we find ourselves looking at the reality of a humble abode—or possibly a broken marriage, as I feared the day Ted left for Vietnam. One woman put it succinctly: "I married an ideal, I got an ordeal, and now I want a new deal."

As we gathered at the riverbank our guide prepared us for the harsh realities of our trip. The rapids were dangerous—so dangerous, in fact, the Canadian government closed the river to rafting after numerous fatalities occurred. Raft Ranch had permission to operate only because of our guide's expertise and international reputation for reliability.

Our only hope of surviving the river, he told us sternly, was to hold on to our paddles and do exactly as he said. He would warn us about any upcoming whirlpools. These turbulent zones can cause a raft to spin in place and make it impossible to paddle back out.

Marriages also can find themselves spinning in an endless downward spiral that can eventually destroy the entire family. Even before Ted left to go overseas, our marriage balanced on the edge of that spiral. He was a workaholic on his way to becoming an alcoholic. As the days passed, my anger—and attempts to control the situation—grew. It took a war and a series of miracles to lead us both to surrender our lives to

Jesus and allow the Holy Spirit to fill us. With him as our expert guide, things began to change.

And change came quickly. Ted resigned his commission, and before we knew it we were on our way to seminary and full-time ministry. Serenely confident, I knew we would have nothing but smooth sailing from that point forward.

Surprise, surprise. Jesus's disciples had to face storms even when their Master was in the boat.

Rough Waters: Conflict Resolution

I want to discuss two stormy situations couples often experience as they travel through the rapids of life. With the wisdom and grace of Christ, we can outmaneuver any rough waters. Jesus told us he would not leave us as orphans (John 14:18) but would send the Holy Spirit who, like an expert river guide, would lead us into radical truth and real solutions.

One of the areas that can lead directly into rough waters for couples—at least those I have counseled over the years—is the way problems are resolved. I can't tell you how many women have cried in my office about how insensitive their husband seems to be. Wives often report that even when they have an unresolved disagreement, their husband still wants to have sex. The husband wants to meet the physical need; the wife wants to resolve the issue emotionally and spiritually first. I explain to these wives that both they and their husband are trying to operate according to the Golden Rule rather than extending it by using the Ephesians Rule as discussed in chapter 4. The diagram on page 239 helps us understand our tendencies as men and women.

As you can see from this behavioral range diagram, women tend to solve problems emotionally and spiritually (from the right side of the diagram) while men want to approach them physically and logically (from the left side of the diagram). Remember, Ephesians 5:33 challenges wives to respect or ad-

Behavior Ranges

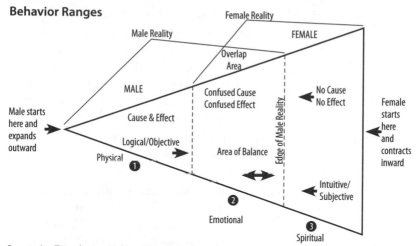

Source: Joe Tanenbaum, *Male and Female Realities: Understanding the Opposite Sex* (Baltimore: Candle Publishing, 1989), 72. Used by permission.

mire their husbands. Men need tangible affirmation because they approach life that way. They want to touch, hold, and see an objective reality. Women tend to have a more inward focus; they respond intuitively and subjectively. That's why Ephesians 5:25 challenges husbands to "love your wives," encouraging them to meet the emotional needs that are a part of God's divine design.

Often, women fail to realize how difficult and unnatural men find it to operate in the emotional and spiritual realm. The dotted line in the diagram, for example, points out that the range of a man's reality usually stops short of the spiritual. The Behavioral Ranges diagram helped me understand why most Christian churches have more women than men who attend. Many religions, including Judaism and Islam, contain physical rituals such as bowing to the east at set times during the day or reciting certain dogma. Men can follow physical requirements like these that clearly prescribe the rules. They identify strongly with the *tangible aspects* of religion.

Christianity, however, is based in *relationship*. Christ died to free us from rules and rituals; he wants an intimate relationship instead. I believe that without a born-again experience, the dotted line on the graph represents reality for most men. As Jesus told Nicodemus, "Unless one is born again he cannot see the kingdom of God" (John 3:3 NASB). Until God awakens a man's spirit, it is almost impossible for him to move into the spiritual realm. As we have said throughout this book, Christian couples have a huge advantage. Since true biblical intimacy is a multidimensional reality, those who grow in their knowledge of Christ should be among the most sexually fulfilled people on the planet.

To help women understand the man's tendency to fix problems by having sex, I point to the book of Genesis: "Then God said, 'Let us make man in our image, in our likeness. . . .' So God created man in his own image, . . . in the image of God he created him; male and female he created them" (Gen. 1:26–27).

God chose to reproduce and reflect himself in mankind; but notice the image is reflected through the male and female coming together. This helps us understand why Satan—who hates both the name and the image of God—tries to keep us apart physically or pervert our sexual union. I tell women that in an ideal world, part of our coming together would include emotional and spiritual unity.

But I don't want them to miss the power of the physical union God designed us to enjoy. When husbands try to resolve conflict through the physical act of sex, they are not being insensitive. They are, in fact, being extremely sensitive to the separation they sense and the desire for restoration by becoming one. I have found when Ted and I disagree, we can resolve the situation emotionally and spiritually, but until we have intercourse, I still sense space between us. I have learned to declare to the enemy that if we have a disagreement in the morning we are having sex that night.

Peter tells us that "love covers a multitude of sins" (1 Pet. 4:8 NLT). The DSRV (Diane's slightly revised version) says, "Love*making* covers a multitude of sins." When husbands and wives grasp this truth, they begin to realize their mate is not the enemy. Instead, the enemy of our souls is the enemy of our marriages—and of our marital intimacy too.

Rough Waters: Unequally Yoked

The second area of struggle occurs when couples are unequally yoked (2 Cor. 6:14). When you're not in the same boat spiritually, you can easily find yourself paddling in opposite directions. Sometimes we think of *unequally yoked* as referring only to couples in which one is a Christ-follower and the other is not. But when both spouses are Christians and one is less willing to grow spiritually than the other, great frustration can occur.

Part of the reason many women find themselves in this situation is what I call *mismatched expectations*. During the dating process, a woman tends to look for a man with potential. She doesn't expect him to stay the same person she met; she expects him to change and grow. A man, on the other hand, tends to marry a woman for who she is rather than who she will become. He can become as frustrated when his wife starts changing as she does when he stays the same.

Because of this problem, I counsel single women to date Christian men who are committed to spiritual growth. But when a wife finds herself unequally yoked, how can she maneuver through the churning rapids of mismatched expectations? I learned early in our Spirit-filled journey that the Holy Spirit is more than willing to give us guidance if we are willing to call upon him.

Although Ted had made incredible progress in his Christian walk, seminary exposed some issues that caught me off guard. We went out with another couple from the seminary one evening and as we were driving home together, Ted made a very prideful remark that stunned and embarrassed me. Now Ted had carried the same pride in the military, but when you're fighting to stay alive in combat, you have to believe you're the best in order to make it home alive. When we spent time with other Marine couples, we often heard prideful talk among the men.

Then life had moved us into a seminary environment in which everyone spoke the language of holiness. Suddenly Ted's pride became a glaring problem he failed to see. All of us (especially wives) are endowed with radar that remains blind to our own issues but zeroes in when it comes to our mate. I started to say something to Ted after dropping off the other couple, but the Holy Spirit cautioned me to be quiet. Later I brought the matter before the Lord. *God, you have to change Ted. His statements were downright embarrassing.*

The Lord's still, small response stunned me. *I don't change people because you're embarrassed.*

But Lord, we're preparing for ministry, and you've called him to be your humble servant. Finally I sensed God's pleasure. Later I realized why. I had switched from praying only according to my selfish desires to praying according to God's calling on Ted's life.

Praying in the Light of His Calling

God has a call on the life of every person who has said yes to him. Paul reminds us, "And we know that in all things God works for the good of those who love him, who have been called according to his purpose" (Rom. 8:28). We often quote the first half of this verse but ignore the final phrase. Praying according to Ted's calling made a difference in my prayer life, in my husband, and especially in me.

Within days of my prayer that God would help Ted walk in humility, he came home declaring he had heard from the Lord about some issues in his life. *Wow, that was a fast answer.* Stunned, I listened as Ted explained more about what God had said. He had instructed Ted to get rid of all his military gear, including his military flight jacket. He had always taken great pride in that jacket, which he wore especially when he rode his motorcycle to attend seminary classes. *That can't be the answer to my prayer. Where will we get the funds to replace such a great jacket?*

I had much more to learn, as you probably recognize. When I pray for change in someone else, God usually starts with me. Christians love to point to the portion of Matthew 7:7 that tells us to ask, seek, and knock. But we tend to skip over the section just a few verses earlier that instructs us to take the beam out of our own eye before we try to remove the speck from our brother's (Matt. 7:5). God had exposed an area of my life that needed to be changed: the fear of not having enough money. I've learned since then that walking by faith will always challenge me to trust God—especially with our finances.

Why did God ask Ted to get rid of his military gear? He began showing me that ever since Ted was a small boy he had wanted to be a man's man—a pilot. In order to attain his goal, pride became a huge part of his life and identity as a man. My original prayer asked God to change Ted's behavior. That would have been like cutting the top off a dandelion. Instead, God wisely dealt with the core issue that had created the pride. He was not cutting off the top; he was pulling it up by the roots.

Not only will God be quick to answer prayers that line up with his calling, but he will also move to protect the calling itself. In Matthew 16:13–19 God reveals to Peter that Jesus is the Christ. A few verses later, when Jesus shares that his calling will require his death on the cross, Peter responds thoughtlessly, "Never, Lord! . . . This shall never happen to you!" Jesus promptly rebukes him, "You do not have in mind the things of God, but the things of men" (Matt. 16:22–23).

I heard the same rebuke from the Lord a number of years later regarding my husband's calling. We were part of a church that used drama as an evangelistic outreach at Christmas and Easter. Ted, as a staff member, was asked to take a significant role in the Christmas drama. I protested because his mother was coming to visit for the holidays. The rehearsal schedule would require him to be away every night for the three weeks before Christmas.

Ted felt God wanted him to take part in the program, but I made things miserable for him each time he left for rehearsal. After only two rehearsals, God spoke a prophetic word in one of our church services. He warned that someone was walking on thin ice because this person knew the will of the Father but was directly opposing his plan.

Immediately I knew God meant that word for me. I changed my heart and supported Ted in his decision. On the other side of Christmas, the Lord challenged me again. This time he said I should not assume I knew the full extent of Ted's calling.

I didn't understand those words until five years later when God called us to East Hill Church. There, Ted became senior pastor and the church became widely known for its use of drama to reach the pre-Christian. Drama and Ted's sermons became intertwined, and God used him mightily. He was free to pursue this calling because God had changed me. Is your unwillingness to allow God to change you preventing your spouse from fulfilling God's calling?

Peter couldn't fully comprehend the cross or its role in Jesus's calling until the day of Pentecost (Acts 2:1–40). Not until he preached to about three thousand who were gathered that day (and added to the church) did he fully comprehend its impact.

Even as I write this chapter, Ted's calling is expanding. He has stepped out of the senior pastor role and into a ministry (Pure Desire) to help churches confront sexual bondage. God is revealing an entirely new dimension of his calling in this season of our lives and challenging me to embrace it too.

Discovering Your Own Calling

When women realize God is eager to answer prayers that line up with the calling upon their husbands' lives, they usually ask how to go about discovering that calling. I believe the first step lies in discovering your own calling.

How do you do that? In my life, I looked at my natural gifts and desires. I had always wanted to be a teacher. I wanted to make learning easy and fun. I remember at an early age convincing most of the neighborhood kids that collecting stamps would be a great idea. I set up tables in our garage, put a map on the wall, and showed them the countries of origin for various stamps. I also had a desire to be a mother. As I look back on my life, raising our children was one of the most fulfilling times I experienced.

If you're unsure of your calling, ask God to reveal it. He has put natural gifts and passions in you to use in your calling.

The second thing I urge you to examine may surprise you: your areas of weakness and wounding. As we allow God to heal those wounds, they become our strengths and often the focus of our ministry. Ted and I would not be working with Pure Desire Ministries today had we not allowed God to pour his strength through our areas of weakness. He can turn your greatest liabilities into kingdom assets.

It took a while, but eventually I realized that in my growing-up years I was never in touch with my emotions. I had to learn how to understand and express what I was feeling. Now I have a new role as a spiritual mom who ministers to and mentors women who need emotional support. Helping to provide healing for others has given me a sense of fulfillment. I know this is the calling God has given me.

In Ted's life, the father wound and his addictions gave him great understanding for those struggling with similar issues. His weaknesses, surrendered to the Lord, have become his greatest strengths. Although he was fatherless, he has become a father to many. As someone who has escaped the web of addiction, he has been used of God to help others caught in the same web.

We often look at our husband and see his problems and weaknesses. God sees him complete, walking in the fullness of the calling he has placed on his life.

As we look back on the Raft Ranch experience, our kids still think it was one of our best family adventures. When we fully surrender to God and allow him to lead us through the rough rapids and whitewater of life, he is faithful to help us reach our destination and to make it a great adventure. He is faithful to help us in our quest to become Sexy Christians.

Appendix 2

Sexy Christians: Man to Man

TED

The setting was a country club in the hills that overlooked the shining, modern city of Hong Kong. I stood to the side of the room as I waited to speak, kicking myself for agreeing to address this group of Chinese Christian businessmen. I knew little about their culture, and I shuddered as I heard the interpreter translate the introduction I was receiving: "Dr. Roberts is a world-renowned expert on sexuality, and he will answer any questions you may have." All the while I was thinking, *Thank God my wife isn't here to dispute that claim.*

My dialogue with the men began slowly, but I soon found myself in familiar territory. I was answering the same questions I had already heard a thousand times from men in the States.

I have since found the same thing to be true no matter where I travel in the world. Men may live in different cultures, but the questions they have about their sexuality as Christ-followers are amazingly similar. Here are some of the questions men around the world have about sex, followed by my answers. I hope you will find something here for you as well.

Is it okay to masturbate?
Every study I have ever read reveals 90 to 95 percent of men have masturbated. (I think the other 5 to 10 percent lied.) Twenty-seven percent of men say they masturbate at least once a week.[1] But we need to place these figures within the context of human sexual development. A survey of sexual behavior in various cultures suggests that, if permitted, most boys and girls will progress from absentminded fingering of their genitals to systematic masturbation by ages six to eight.[2]

So masturbation is not the unpardonable sin but a very powerful experience. As we have discussed, experiencing a climax is definitely a brain-impacting event. For most individuals, especially women, inducing a climax through masturbation is much easier than experiencing one while making love with their spouse. But men are the ones who can easily get trapped in masturbation.

I have discovered through my years of counseling men that premature ejaculation is a common problem. This is the inability to control one's orgasm long enough to complete intercourse. In other words, ejaculation occurs prior to penetration. The man who can avoid premature ejaculation has developed the ability to avoid focusing on himself long enough to bring his wife to a satisfying sexual experience. Failing to accomplish that can lead to male performance anxiety because the man senses his wife is not fulfilled. For many men, the pattern of quick release learned through masturbation has totally messed up their sex lives and made real intimacy impossible.

Most men can trace their history of masturbation back to their early teen years. These times of masturbation were quick and powerful, deeply imprinting in their brains the pattern of rapidly reaching orgasm after arousal. This pattern becomes so ingrained that it persists in marriage. The man in this situation has trained himself to focus too much on the orgasmic and sensual effects of lovemaking and not enough on the relationship.

When a man asks me if masturbation is okay, I ask him what he is thinking about when he masturbates. An awkward silence ensues as he comprehends what my question implies. Lustful fantasies thrive and grow in the mental world of masturbation. Even a married man is almost never thinking of his wife while he masturbates. Instead, he is responding to some pornographic image stored in his mind.

Earlier I referred to a survey of children in various cultures that stated, "If permitted, boys and girls progress from absentminded fingering of their genitals to systematic masturbation." The key words are *absentminded* and *if permitted*. Initially our interest in masturbation is absentminded, but soon, if permitted, it can begin to rule our mind. One difference between a boy and a man is the boy has to have what he wants *right away*. A man will delay gratification for a higher cause. When it comes to masturbation, the higher cause is the quality of intimacy he will experience with his wife.

What's so wrong with watching porn on the internet?

I can hardly believe it when someone asks me this question. But the younger he is, the less he seems to recognize the problem with the behavior. The simple answer: porn devastates a healthy marriage or a single person's life as a Christ follower. The internet is a great accelerator of what happens when someone watches a porn movie. The web has become the number-one sex education tool in our society. And this same tool is now one of the main activities for kids as they do their homework.[3]

Let me give you four reasons the internet has become so powerful:

1. *Anonymity*: Viewers of porn feel as though no one knows what they are doing. A simple click of the mouse puts them in contact with a highly erotic environment. The process itself isolates them from those closest to them. This gives the illusion that sex on the internet is impersonal and doesn't hurt anyone else, which only increases their sense of isolation.

2. *Cost*: The relative cost of the internet is very low. A hardcore pornographic magazine can cost over thirty dollars. But for the same amount of money, an internet connection affords the viewer with an endless stream of pornographic material from free sites alone.

3. *Intensity*: The internet is a high-tech way of getting a quick fix, but it is far more powerful. Al Cooper and other researchers in this area have described cybersex as the crack cocaine of compulsive sexual behavior. Internet sexual stimulation has the capacity to go beyond our biological limits. No partner can compete with the internet. In fact, people can get so stimulated that online sex feels better than the real-life version. The marketing loops used by the porn sites create so many options that viewers can access information about unresolved sexual issues in their lives. They can use this virtual means to explore areas they've wondered about or things about which they have fantasized. Sexual addiction through cybersex escalates very rapidly once it has begun, and it typically extends to non-internet behaviors. Sexual addicts in recovery have reported internet sex as one of the primary reasons they relapse.[4]

4. *Dominance*: The internet has become an integral part of our lives, so it is nearly impossible to avoid. That means the decision never to use it again is not an option for most people. Our world has become internet-interactive—another facet of the power of cybersex. Unlike pornographic magazines or movies that don't respond to us, the internet does.

It frequently prompts us for information, which makes it feel more real than the other types of pornographic media. When you add pornographic chat rooms, strippers, live sex acts with video streaming that responds to viewers' requests, and sharing of pornographic pictures on cell phones, you're dealing with a media that has incredible power to destroy.

Is it okay to have oral sex in marriage?

If you've ever read the Song of Songs, you realize right up front that this couple wants to experience the full beauty of the sexual relationship as designed by God. One thing I've learned is to let the Word of God—not the opinions of humans—define the boundaries of healthy sexuality. This is true whether the opinions come from the pulpit or from the latest hot counseling book. We must remain open to input from others, of course, but history reveals the church has frequently drawn sexual boundaries out of fear, not fulfillment.

One of the great things about studying the Hebrew language is the way it allows us to understand the true passion and eroticism of the words in the Song of Songs. Listen to what Shulamith says she wants to do once she and her beloved get married: "Like an apple tree among the trees in the forest, so is my beloved among the young men. I want to sit in his shadow. His fruit tastes sweet to me" (Song of Songs 2:3 GW).

Notice that the bride is not commenting on the quality of the king's apple orchard. This is a poetic reference to oral sex. Once again, Solomon's bride is comfortable with her sexuality but adventurous at the same time. Understanding the original language helps explain why Solomon ran down the aisle with a smile on his face at the wedding. And it helps us reexamine some of our decisions as well.

Frequently, a deeper issue lies behind the question of whether oral sex is okay. The husband wants his wife to engage in oral sex and she is closed to the idea. He asks the question to try to gain leverage for his position in order to get his wife to give him what he wants.

Similar disagreements occurred during New Testament times. In his writings, the apostle Paul gives an incredible principle for fulfillment: *it must be mutual* (1 Cor. 7:3–5)—it's not about me. Frequently, men in particular get the idea that a certain sexual act will enliven their sex life. Unfortunately, that idea often comes from the pornographic air we tend to breathe in our culture. For the husband, that sexual act becomes an obsession, which takes it into the realm of sin.

Instead, both husband and wife need to discover new sexual territory together. "But my wife won't risk anything sexually," the husband responds.

If I sense he'll receive my teaching, I tell him, "If you meet her emotional needs in the bedroom . . . if you love her through her wounds from the past . . . if you give her a safe place to process her pain, even if it takes a long time . . . if you love your wife this way, she'll leave you in the dust sexually. She'll be the one saying, 'Come on, big boy, let's try this!'" Men, focus on loving your wife deeply, not on pushing her into some new type of sexual activity.

Why are we having so many sexual problems in our marriage?

Here's the shocking truth: in a sex-saturated society in which we even have Christian books on how to have a great sex life, many of our marriages are not doing well sexually. In 1992 the National Health and Social Life Survey was conducted (an epidemiological study of 1,749 women and 1,410 men between the ages of eighteen and fifty-nine). The study revealed 43 percent of women and 31 percent of men reported having a sexual problem *in the prior year*.[5] This means many women aren't having a particularly good time in bed—and it's doubtful their partners are either. The report underlines the fact that there are many nervous people trying to do what supposedly comes easily and naturally, but it's not happening either way.

My counseling experience suggests the figures reported in the survey are actually an underestimate. The report also uncovered the fact that a quarter of all women report having difficulty reaching orgasm.[6] One out of four women lie there wondering if they'll reach orgasm and worrying about how their partners will respond if they don't. Instead of relaxing in bed, lots of folks are acting instead.

Recent PET scans of the female brain help us understand how women can be caught up in such a struggle.[7] The scans showed when women reached orgasm, something unexpected happened. There was decreased activity in the lateral orbito-frontal cortex—an area that governs self-control over basic desires such as sex. (Stick with me; it will all make sense in a moment.) There was also a dip in excitation in the Dorso-medial prefrontal cortex, which governs moral reasoning and social judgment. In other words, orgasm yielded a release of tension and inhibition.

Conversely, at the moment of orgasm the limbic region (which produces oxytocin, the bonding hormone) lit up because oxytocin levels jumped fourfold. Here is what the researchers said was the bottom line: "Fear and anxiety need to be avoided at all costs if a woman wished to have an orgasm; we knew that, but now we can see it happening in the depths of the brain."[8]

The research makes it crystal clear: what we need is not some new sexual technique or suggestions about how to make love in the dining room instead of the bedroom. (Of course if you want to, go for it. Just be careful of the dishes!) What we need instead is safe, caring, and honest communication about our own woundedness. That will lead to real intimacy.

We are dying for this type of biblical relationship. Sexual problems in marriages are gifts that tell us God is challenging us to dig deeper into him. Remember, intimacy is getting *up close and uncomfortable* with another imperfect human being. Instead of trying to find ways to deal with the sexual boredom we may be experiencing as a couple, we need to dig deep in Christ and allow him to heal us so deeply that we can passionately give to one another.

I am struggling with pornography. Should I tell my wife?

This has to be one of the most frequently voiced questions I hear in private. I consider the answer a no-brainer: yes. You are only as sick as your secrets, my friend. If you ever want to get free from this monster eating at your soul, you must stop having sexual secrets. Christ didn't die so you could die slowly from the inside out.

Now comes the interesting part: How do I tell her? Allow me to give you several life- and marriage-saving suggestions:

1. *Become part of an accountability group.* You must become part of a men's group that really knows what it's doing when it comes to sexual addiction (such as a Pure Desire men's group). In other words, you don't need the typical men's accountability group that is not a true accountability group but a Christian performance group. I recently spoke with a pastor who was overseeing another pastor's restoration process after a moral failure. I asked how they were helping the man, and the pastor told me, "Oh, we've developed an accountability group for him."

"Oh, great," I replied. I then asked, "How does it work?"

"Well, the ex-pastor reports to the group once a week."

Sensing my blood pressure rising, I asked, "Does anyone in this group have any real experience or clinical ability in dealing with sexual addiction?"

"Not really," he responded. "He just reports to us once a week."

"That is not an accountability group; that is a performance group. In other words, all you do is check to see if he has messed up again. A true accountability group helps a man find the resources to bridge the gap between where he is and where he longs to be."

2. *Tell the whole truth.* Have someone who knows how to do this help you plan how and when you will tell your wife

the whole truth. Don't tell her half the truth or part of the truth. She needs the whole truth right up front in order to have any hope of believing you again.

3. *Help your wife find appropriate support.* Your wife will need to meet with a qualified counselor or join a Pure Desire women's group. Her world has just fallen apart. What she only suspected has now become reality. She's going to need lots of support to walk through the pain if your marriage is going to make it.

And a special note: *don't make your wife your accountability partner.* She needs to be your wife, not your sheriff. She'll never learn to trust you again if you constantly ask her to hold you accountable. You must get healed to the place where *you* hold yourself accountable.

4. *Join the battle.* It will take some time for you to learn to walk in true sexual health. But don't despair; your wound can become a great point of strength. Every weekend there are millions of men sitting in a church pew dying, and their marriages are also slowly dying. They're not experiencing the sexual, emotional, relational, and spiritual fulfillment Christ died to bring. They're waiting for you to walk out of hell into health so you can lead them out of hell too.

Sexy Christians make a difference in the lives of those around them—man to man.

Acknowledgments

TED

Like a stunned Oscar-receiving starlet who doesn't know when to stop, some acknowledgments can be long-winded and unreadable. Take heart; I will come right to the point.

To the folks of East Hill Church: I can't thank you enough. For twenty-four years you encouraged me as I stumbled, fumbled, and grew in my ability as a counselor. Now as I look back I realize I was the one being trained by you.

To the Pure Desire Ministries International Staff, who decided to walk into the unknown with me. Your support and commitment gave me hope to try again and again. Thank you.

To Dr. Jack Hayford, who has believed in me through the years (though at times I am sure he thought I was a bit crazy), thank you.

To Dr. Glenn Burris, my boss, who believed in me for so long when many couldn't accept the existence of sexual addiction in the church or the need for *Sexy Christians*, thank you.

To Dr. Patrick Carnes, who in so many ways became a mentor and personal friend in this amazing journey of helping people come to sexual health, thank you.

To Christopher Ferebee, who led me through the serpentine intricacies of endless pages of contracts, thank you.

To Marti Pieper, who took our simple literary efforts and turned them into something God will use as an instrument to heal thousands of marriages, thank you.

To Chad Allen, who healed my experience of dealing with publishers and who understands the problem of the hurting multitudes within the church, thank you.

To my kids and grandkids, who have healed me in ways I can't express and helped me understand what a healthy family is all about, thank you.

To my wife, the love of my life, who loved me into the kingdom of God and has stood beside me through thick and thin (and some of the thick times were really thick), thank you.

To my Lord, Friend, Ultimate Mentor, and Holy God, Jesus Christ, who raised me from the brink of death to life—real life. I will thank you all the days of my life!

Notes

Foreword

1. Timothy Keller, *The Prodigal God: Recovering the Heart of the Christian Faith* (New York: Dutton Adult, 2008).

Chapter 1 Sexy Christians: An Oxymoron?

1. Liza Featherstone, "You, Me and Porn Make Three," *Psychology Today* (September/October 2005): 83–86.
2. Patrick Carnes, "Women and Sex Addiction," *Counselor* (June 2006): 34–37.
3. "Internet Pornography Statistics: 2003," www.healthymind.com/s-porn-stats.html (accessed February 2, 2009).

Chapter 2 The Magic of the Moment

1. Celine Dion, "It's All Coming Back to Me Now," composed by Jim Steinman, *Falling Into You*, Universal Music Publishing Group, 1996.
2. David Barlow and Mark Durand, *Abnormal Psychology: An Integrative Approach* (Belmont, CA: Wadsworth Publishing, 2005), 41–44, 306–8.
3. W. F. Arndt and F. W. Gingrich, *A Greek-English Lexicon of the New Testament and Other Early Christian Literature* (Chicago: University of Chicago Press, 1957), 404.
4. Louis Cozolino, *The Neuroscience of Human Relationships* (New York: W. W. Norton, 2006), 139–45.

Chapter 3 Strangers and Aliens

1. Marcus Buckingham and Curt Coffman, *First, Break All the Rules: What the World's Greatest Managers Do Differently* (New York: Simon and Schuster, 1999), 80.
2. www.thinkexist.com/quotes/raquel_welch (accessed February 24, 2009).
3. Daniel Amen, *Sex on the Brain: 12 Lessons to Enhance Your Love Life* (New York: Harmony, 2007), 3–22.
4. Cozolino, *Neuroscience of Human Relationships*, 139–45.
5. Cris Evatt, *He and She: A Lively Guide to Understanding the Opposite Sex* (Newburyport, MA: Conari Press, 1992), 124.
6. Louann Brizendine, *The Female Brain* (New York: Broadway Books, 2006), 12.
7. Elizabeth Vargas, "The Truth Behind Women's Brains," www.abcnews. go.com/2020/story?id=2504460&page=2 (accessed February 24, 2009).
8. Ibid.
9. Ibid.
10. Shaunti Feldhahn and Jeff Feldhahn, *For Men Only: A Straightforward Guide to the Inner Lives of Women* (Portland: Multnomah, 2006), 53–57.

Chapter 4 Code Talkers

1. Harrison Lapahie Jr., "Diné Bizaad Yee Atah Naayéé' Yik'eh Deesdlíí" ("The Navajo Language Assisted the Military Forces to Defeat the Enemy"), www.lapahie. com/NavajoCodeTalker.cfm (accessed January 22, 2009).
2. Darcy Luadzers, *The Ten Minute Sexual Solution* (Long Island City, NY: Hatherleigh Press, 2006), 4–5.
3. Shaunti Feldhahn, *For Women Only: What You Need to Know about the Inner Lives of Men* (Portland: Multnomah, 2004), 68, 93.
4. Ibid., 100.
5. Feldhahn and Feldhahn, *For Men Only*, 30, 38–39.
6. Barbara De Angelis, *What Women Want Men to Know: The Ultimate Book about Love, Sex and Relationships for You—and the Man You Love* (New York: Hyperion, 2001), 310–11.
7. Ibid.

Chapter 5 Hidden Enemy

1. Patricia Leonard, "Life in These United States," *Reader's Digest*, March 2005, 201.
2. David Schnarch, *Passionate Marriage: Keeping Love and Intimacy Alive in Emotionally Committed Relationships* (New York: W. W. Norton, 1997), 122.
3. A. T. Robertson, *Word Pictures in the New Testament*, vol. 4 (Nashville: Broadman Press, 1931), 540.

Chapter 6 Catch and Release

1. Gary Richmond, *A View from the Zoo: Super Speedsters* (Irvine, CA: Randolf Productions, 2007), VHS 1–57919–1258, ASIN: B000W4ZAPY.

2. William Barclay, *New Testament Words* (Louisville: Westminster Press, 1974), 116–18.

3. Schnarch, *Passionate Marriage*, 40.

4. Robert J. Levin and Amy Levin, "Sexual Pleasure: The Surprising Preferences of 100,000 Women," *Redbook*, September 1975, 51–58.

5. Edward Laumann, John Gagnon, Robert Michael, and Stuart Michaels, *The Organization of Sexuality: Sexual Practices in the United States* (Chicago: University of Chicago Press, 1994), 363–65.

6. Robert Michael, John Gagnon, and Edward Laumann, *Sex in America: A Definitive Survey* (Boston: Little, Brown and Company, 1994), 130.

Chapter 7 Getting Up Off the Floor

1. Elizabeth Williamson, "Lack of Teen Maturity May Explain Teen Crash Rate," *Washington Post*, February 2005, sec. A, 1.

2. R. A. Lanives, P. C. Williamson, and R. S. Menon Williamson, "Brain Activation during Script-Driven Imagery-Induced Dissociative Responses in PTSD," *Biological Psychiatry* 52:305–311.

3. Centers for Disease Control and Prevention, "Adverse Childhood Experiences Study," www.cdc.gov/nccdphp/ace/findings.htm (accessed April 10, 2008).

4. Y. Shoda, W. Mischel, and P. K. Peake, "Predicting Adolescent Cognitive and Self-Regulatory Competencies from Preschool Delay of Gratification," *Developmental Psychology* 26, no. 6 (1990): 978–86. Referenced in "Kagan Structures for Emotional Intelligence," *Kagan Online Magazine*, Fall 2001, www.kaganonline.com/KaganClub/FreeArticles/ASK14.html (accessed April 14, 2008).

5. Rick Renner, *Sparkling Gems from the Greek* (Tulsa: Teach All Nations, 2003), 77.

6. Jim Collins, *Good to Great: Why Some Companies Make the Leap . . . and Others Don't* (New York: HarperCollins, 2001), 85.

Chapter 8 Clipped Wings

1. Anonymous, email to Diane Roberts, used by permission.

2. S. Brody and T. H. Kruger, "The Post-Orgasmic Prolactin Increase Following Intercourse Is Greater than Following Masturbation and Suggests Greater Satiety," *Biological Psychology* 71, no. 3:312–15.

3. Anthony Wolf, *Why Can't You Shut Up? How We Ruin Relationships—How Not To* (New York: Ballantine, 2006), 102.

4. John Gottman, *The Seven Principles of Making Marriage Work* (Philadelphia: Three Rivers Press, 2000), 130.

5. Rollo May, *Love and Will* (New York: W. W. Norton, 1969), 87.

6. Carnes, "Women and Sex Addiction," 34–39.

Chapter 9 One Hot Couple

1. John Woodbridge, *Great Leaders of the Christian Church* (Chicago: Moody Press, 1988), 56.

2. Roy Battenhouse, ed., *A Companion to the Study of St. Augustine* (Grand Rapids: Baker, 1979), 382.

3. Lisa Harper, *What Every Girl Wants: A Portrait of Perfect Love and Intimacy in the Song of Solomon* (Carol Stream, IL: Tyndale, 2006), 73.

4. Edward Goodrick and John Kohlenberger, *NIV Exhaustive Concordance* (Grand Rapids: Zondervan, 1990), 1466.

5. Helen Fisher, "Lust, Attraction, Attachment: Biology and Evolution of the Three Primary Emotion Systems for Mating, Reproduction, and Parenting," *Journal of Sex Education and Therapy* 25, no.1:96–102.

6. A. Wise, "Psychomotor Stimulant Properties of Addictive Drugs," in *The Mesocorticolimbic Dopamine System*, ed. P. W. Kalinas and C. B. Nemeroff, Annals of the New York Academy of Sciences 537 (New York: New York Academy of Sciences, 1988), 228–34.

7. Patrick Carnes, *Facing the Shadow*, 2nd ed. (Scottsdale, AZ: Gentle Path Press, 2005), 28.

8. R. A. Ruden, *The Craving Brain: The Biobalance Approach to Controlling Addictions* (New York: Harper Collins, 1997), 32–103.

Chapter 10 One Cold Bed

1. Gary Rosberg and Barbara Rosberg with Ginger Kolbaba, *The 5 Sex Needs of Men and Women* (Carol Stream, IL: Tyndale, 2006).

2. Ibid.

3. Gottman, *Seven Principles*, 17.

4. Louis Cozolino, *The Neuroscience of Psychotherapy* (W. W. Norton, 2002), 78.

5. David Schnarch, *Resurrecting Sex* (New York: Quill, 2003), 34.

6. Gottman, *Seven Principles*, 11.

Chapter 11 Fire-Starters

1. Alfred Ells, *One-Way Relationships* (Nashville: Thomas Nelson, 1990), 189–93.

2. John Piper, "Hell Has Never Produced a Single Pleasure," www.desiringgod.org/Blog/1940_never_produced_a_single_pleasure.

3. Luadzers, *Ten Minute Sexual Solution*, 11.

4. Ibid., 37.

5. Ted Roberts, *Pure Desire* (Ventura, CA: Regal Books, 1999), 265.

6. Diane Roberts, *Betrayed Heart Manual* (Gresham, OR: East Hill Church, 2000), 15.

7. Anonymous email to Diane Roberts, used by permission.

Chapter 12 The Fiery Mountain of Intimacy

1. A. N. Schore, "Early Superego Development: The Emergence of Shame and Narcissistic Affect Regulation in the Practicing Period," *Psychoanalysis and Contemporary Thought* (1991): 14, 187–250.

2. John Bradshaw, *Healing the Shame That Binds You* (Deerfield Beach, FL: Health Communications, 1993), 96.

3. A. N. Schore, *Affect Regulation and the Origin of the Self: The Neurobiology of Emotional Development* (Hillsdale, NJ: Erlbaum, 1994), 26–38.

4. K. A. Brennan and P. R. Shaver, "Dimensions of Adult Attachment, Affect Regulation and Romantic Relationship Functioning," in *Personality and Social Psychology Bulletin* 21, no. 3 (1995): 267–83.

5. Sarah McLachlan, "Angel," Sony/ATV Songs LLC and Tyde Music, 1997.

6. Ibid.

Chapter 13 The Wonder of It All

1. Tobin Perry, "Survey Says the Average Toolbox Reader May Have a Sexual Addiction," http://legacy.pastors.com/RWMT/article.asp?ID=344&ArtID=11066 (accessed February 20, 2009).

2. National Association for Children of Alcoholics, "Children of Alcoholics: Important Facts," www.meccaservices.com/pdfs/childrenalcoholics.pdf (accessed February 21, 2009).

3. Patrick Carnes, "Old Temptation: New Technology, Pornography and the Internet in Today's World," www.iitap.com/documents/ARTICLE_Old%20Temptation%20New%20Technology.pdf (accessed February 21, 2009).

4. Carole Zawid, *Sexual Health: A Nurse's Guide* (Albany, NY: Delmar Publishers, Western School Press, 1993), 46.

5. Pure Desire men's groups are healing and recovery groups based on Ted Roberts's book *Pure Desire* and associated materials, www.puredesire.org.

6. Harville Hendrix, *Getting the Love You Want: A Guide for Couples* (Geneva, IL: Holt Books, 2007), 42–89.

7. Patrick Carnes, *Contrary to Love: Helping the Sexual Addict* (Minneapolis: CompCare Publishers, 1989), 103–31.

Appendix 2 Sexy Christians: Man to Man

1. Edward Laumann, *The Social Organization of Sexuality: Sexual Practices in the United States* (Chicago: University of Chicago Press, 1997), 41, table 3:1.

2. Janet Hyde and John DeLamater, *Understanding Human Sexuality*, 9th ed. (New York: McGraw-Hill Humanities/Social Sciences/Languages, 2006), 262.

3. Patrick Carnes, *The 90-Day Prep* (Scottsdale, AZ: Gentle Path Press, 2006), 27.

4. Ibid., 28.

5. Michael, Gagnon, and Laumann, *Sex in America*.

6. Janniko Georgiadis, "Regional Cerebral Blood Flow Changes Associated with Clitorally Induced Orgasm in Healthy Women," *European Journal of Neuroscience* 24, no.11:3305–16.

7. Martin Portner, "The Orgasmic Mind," *Scientific American* (April/May 2008).

8. Ibid., 71.

Sexy Christians: Tell Me More!

TED AND DIANE

How can I become a Sexy Christian?
Pick up the *Sexy Christians Workbook* (Baker Books, 2010) to help personalize our teaching for your own life and marriage. Designed for use by individuals, couples, or small groups, it's available in bookstores, online, or wherever Christian books are sold. And make sure to visit our online home: www.sexychristians.com. It's the place to order additional books and other Sexy Christians materials, download video podcasts of our teaching, and become part of the continuing Sexy Christians conversation.

How can I attend a Sexy Christians Seminar?
Check out our speaking schedule online at www.sexy christians.com or www.puredesire.org, the online home of Pure Desire Ministries International (PDMI). If you don't see anything in your area, check out "Host a Seminar" and invite us soon. (Make sure you type www.sexychristians.com exactly to avoid a potentially dangerous site.)

I'm struggling with a sexual addiction. Where can I go for help?

Go to www.puredesire.org and click on "find a Pure Desire group." This page will help you find PDMI affiliates that offer Pure Desire groups for men and women. Click on your state to find local groups. If you need more help, view our materials online or call our ministry office at 1-503-489-0235.

I am a pastor or other large-group leader. How can I host a Sexy Christians Seminar?

Check out the information online at www.sexychristians.com, "Host a Seminar." Fill out the information request and a PDMI staff member will contact you soon. You can also email us at kathyw@puredesire.org.

I teach a small group or adult Sunday school class. Can Sexy Christians be taught in that setting?

In a word, yes. We recommend our *Sexy Christians Workbook* as a guide. It contains questions, practical applications, and leaders' tips that are perfect for use in a Bible study or other small group. You can also adapt the Home Plays from *Sexy Christians* for use with your small group. Check out www.sexychristians.com, "Leader Tips," for more leaders' helps. And contact Direct2Church (a division of Baker Publishing Group) for information on orders and special group pricing: www.direct2church.com, 1-800-877-2665.

Dr. Ted Roberts likes to say he was "drafted into the pastorate" from his career as a Marine fighter pilot. During his years as senior pastor of East Hill Church in Gresham, Oregon, the church grew to more than 6,000 members. President and cofounder of Pure Desire Ministries International, Ted is a certified Sex Addiction Therapist whose previous books include *Pure Desire, Seven Pillars of Freedom, For Men Only, Living Life Boldly, Going Deeper,* and *Failing Forward.* Ted is a sought-after speaker who, with his wife Diane, travels across the globe to lead Sexy Christians Conferences.

Diane Roberts provides the perfect balance for her husband in both marriage and ministry. Cofounder of Pure Desire Ministries International, she served alongside Ted as women's ministry director, pastor, and counselor at East Hill Church for more than twenty years. Author of *Betrayed Heart, Betrayal and Beyond: Healing for Broken Trust,* and *Accept No Substitutes* and contributing author of *Pure Desire,* Diane's humor, insights, and experience combine to make her a popular speaker and dynamic coleader of Sexy Christians Conferences. She and Ted have two grown children and four grandchildren.

This book can change your life and your marriage.

Sexy Christians Workbook **is the ultimate resource to transform your relationship.** Designed for use by individuals, couples, and small groups, this companion workbook will help you fully discover what it means to be a Sexy Christian.

Visit www.puredesire.org for more information.

Available wherever books are sold.

Direct 2 Church
○ Resources for Christian Communities

For case quantity discounts of **30–50% off** the regular retail price for your church or group, please visit www.direct2church.com or email us at Direct2Church@BakerPublishingGroup.com.

But it is only the beginning ...

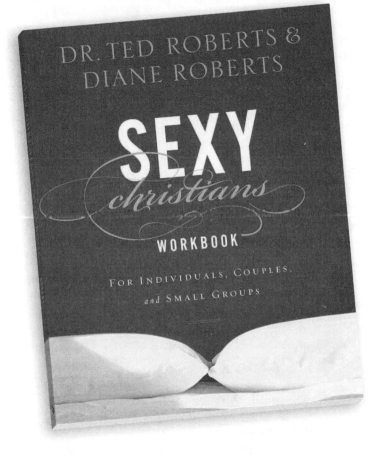